81-1211

PN
1785   Renaissance drama.   New
R4   series.
v.12

JUL   2000

JUN   2004

JUN 09
JUN 0
JUL X X 2015

RENAISSANCE DRAMA

New Series XII ❧ 1981

Renaissance Drama

New Series XII

Essays on Dramatic Technique

Edited by Alan C. Dessen

Northwestern University Press

EVANSTON 1981

The illustration on the front cover is from Andrea Vesalius, *De humani corporis fabrica* (1543), p. 164. Reproduced by courtesy of The Newberry Library.

The illustration on the back cover is "The Devil Applying Cosmetics," from Stephen Hertford, *The Roxburghe Ballads* (1890), p. 128. Reproduced by permission of The Huntington Library, San Marino, California.

Publication of this volume was made possible by a grant from the College of Arts and Sciences, Northwestern University.

Editorial Note

RENAISSANCE DRAMA, an annual publication, provides a forum for scholars in various parts of the globe: wherever the drama of the Renaissance is studied. Coverage, so far as subject matter is concerned, is not restricted to any single national theater. The chronological limits of the Renaissance are interpreted liberally, and space is available for essays on precursors, as well as on the use of Renaissance themes by later writers. Editorial policy favors articles of some scope. Essays that are exploratory in nature, that are concerned with critical or scholarly methodology, that raise new questions or embody fresh approaches to perennial problems are particularly appropriate for a publication that originated from the proceedings of the Modern Language Association Conference on Research Opportunities in Renaissance Drama.

In recent years (as often reflected by the essays in this journal), scholars and critics have dealt extensively with problems of "meaning" in Renaissance plays. Considerably less attention, however, has been paid to the ways in which characters, images, or motifs are presented to the reader or spectator. The question "what does it mean?" remains far more popular than such questions as "how does it mean?" or "how does it work?"

For this volume, the Guest Editor therefore sought essays that dealt with problems in dramatic technique—with questions of "how?" As might be expected (given the many available senses of "technique" and the many different ways of raising such questions), the six essays that follow form no neat pattern. Thus, several of the authors focus upon motifs that recur in different plays and contexts. Ranging widely through the plays of Shakespeare and his contemporaries, Marjorie Garber demonstrates the ubiquitous presence, in comedy as well as tragedy, of *memento mori* figures and notes the telling uses to which such a traditional *topos* could be put. Working with another widespread but less familiar motif, Annette Drew-Bear shows how often tragic dramatists introduced scenes and speeches involving cosmetics and face-painting to characterize social, political, or sexual corruption. Both authors pull together a large number of related scenes and situations in order to enhance our understanding of how Elizabethan dramatists used and developed key images or motifs.

Other authors tackle problems in technique that arise from the gaps between us and the original Renaissance audiences. In a provocative essay (certain to elicit strong responses from "psychological" critics), Robert Hellenga draws upon anthropology, the history of psychology, and his own reading of some major plays to argue against the imposition of a modern sense of "identity" and "reality" upon Elizabethan characters. For him, a modern experience of self (as private and autonomous) can prevent us from seeing a distinctive Elizabethan sense of self (as social and partici-patory), thereby leading to a fruitless search for the "real" person behind the mask of such figures as Hamlet, Othello, and the Duchess of Malfi. In practical theatrical terms, R. B. Graves provides a careful study of lighting effects in the indoor and outdoor theaters (he finds no significant differ-ences) and argues, among other things, that the many candles and torches cited in the plays are important not for any light they cast (negligible in a daylight performance), but for the practical or conventional signals they conveyed—in particular, the information provided through the kind of lighting instrument being used. In very different ways, both of these authors ask us to readjust our expectations and our sense of "conventions" in order to appreciate more fully the original experience.

Working with yet another sense of "technique," Marion Trousdale treats the plays of Shakespeare and others as texts written for oral perfor-mance, with particular emphasis upon oral formulas (an approach that has suggestive implications for the study of iterative imagery). Joan Marx, the only one of these authors to focus upon one play, then demonstrates how Peele in *The Old Wives' Tale* gains his distinctive effects by slipping suddenly from folk tale to romance to folk ritual to farce. And to assuage the modernist who may feel somewhat left out owing to the consistent historical emphasis of these essays, Michael Shapiro in his review article treats some recent contributions to one of the newest and liveliest forms of Shakespearean criticism—the emphasis upon metadramatic or self-reflexive techniques.

As a group, these essays provide no combined assault upon the problem of "how?" yet each author in a distinctive way asks us to reconsider our approach to character or imagery or genre or convention or the nature of performance. To borrow from that scholar-critic Polonius, "though this be madness, yet there is method in't."

The subject of *Renaissance Drama* XIII will be Drama and Society. The editor solicits papers in any area of this broad subject, ranging from views of the historical and social contexts of drama, to studies of political drama and masque, to consideration of society within plays. Special consideration will be given to papers of wide-ranging interest among different dramatists and among different national traditions. Papers should be sent to the editor at Department of English, Northwestern University, Evanston, Illinois 60201. Prospective contributors are requested to follow the recommendations of the *MLA Style Sheet* (revised edition) in preparing manuscripts.

Contents

RENAISSANCE DRAMA

New Series **XII** ✍ 1981

"Remember Me": Memento Mori Figures in Shakespeare's Plays

MARJORIE GARBER

> HAMLET
> My father—methinks I see my father.
> HORATIO
> Where, my lord?
> HAMLET
> In my mind's eye, Horatio.
> . . . .
> HORATIO
> My lord, I think I saw him yesternight.
> (*Hamlet,* I.ii. 184–189)[1]

I F SHAKESPEARE'S PLAY *Hamlet* were a comedy, this exchange would call for what is known in the trade as a "double take"—in fact, two double takes, one by each actor. Hamlet speaks in what seem to be safely metaphoric and prophetic terms—"methinks I see my father . . . In my mind's eye"—but Horatio's factual rejoinder—"I think I saw him yesternight"—instantly undercuts that rhetorical safety, and turns the conversation from the visionary to the visual. In doing so Horatio—and with him, Hamlet—contemplates the crossing of two thresholds—one between life and death, the other between the literal and the metaphorical. In the dramatic architecture of Shakespeare's plays, as I will argue, these two thresholds are frequently twinned or interchangeable: the literal appearance of a *memento mori*, a physical figure or image of death, often intrudes

1. All textual references are to *The Riverside Shakespeare*, ed. G. Blakemore Evans (Boston, 1974).

3

itself upon the developing dramatic action, and alters the understanding of the onstage spectator—and his offstage counterpart as well.

There is perhaps no better place to start such an argument than with the Ghost in *Hamlet*, and in particular with his departing cry, "Adieu, adieu, adieu! remember me" (I.v.91). I would like to suggest that these words are not only an invitation to revenge but also a more generalized *memento mori* sentiment, directly proleptic to Hamlet's literal interview with a skull in the graveyard, and later transmuted into his dying request to Horatio, "in this harsh world draw thy breath in pain, / To tell my story" (v.ii.348–349). The injunction to "remember me" in fact serves as a conundrum for Hamlet, a text he must unpack and interpret; in a sense, that act of interpretation *is* the dramatic action of the play. Three times in Act I, scene v, Hamlet repeats the Ghost's command: "Remember thee!" (l. 95); "Remember thee!" (l. 97), "Now to my word: / It is, 'Adieu, adieu! remember me'" (ll. 110–111). But despite this mnemonic itera- tion, he does not fully understand his charge. The command to revenge is certainly present in the Ghost's phrase, but the heart of the play concerns not the eventual—and almost anticlimactic—dispatching of Claudius, but Hamlet's own meditations on the nature of life and the limits of mortality. "Remember me," rightly interpreted, is the proverbial phrase of the speaking skull in the *memento mori* tradition: it is, therefore, a reminder of every man's death, a reminder to Hamlet of his own death as well as that of his father; it is in fact a summons to the graveyard, where Hamlet, holding aloft the skull of Yorick, holds, "as 'twere, a mirror up to nature."

Not only in *Hamlet*, but throughout Shakespeare's plays, there occur *memento mori* figures of this type, iconographic and dramatized figures that personate death, often in a startling or shocking way. Such figures repre- sent a literalization or unmetaphoring of themes and problems intrinsic to the plays in which they appear; in addition, they serve to frame and deepen the dramatic action, offering a kind of "tragic relief" against which the entire action of the play may be measured.

I take the word "unmetaphoring" here from Rosalie Colie, who defines it simply and clearly: "an author who treats a conventionalized figure of speech," she says, "as if it were a description of actuality is unmetaphoring that figure." As one of her illustrative examples she cites Shakespeare's "transforming a standard prop in the tableaux of noble melancholy into the specific skull of a dead friend."[2] What I am talking about here may be called either unmetaphoring or literalization, but because it deals most specifically with the summoning of deathly *figures*, actual characters in the play, I should prefer to call it "reification." "What, has this *thing* appeared again to-night?" (I.i.21).

Literary and folkloric precedents for this dramatic technique were certainly available to Shakespeare—for example, in Chaucer's *Pardoner's Tale*, or in the medieval topos of the three living and the three dead. The tale of the "appointment in Samarra" is another example of this popular genre. But the most readily available examples of *memento mori* were to be found in the works of painters, engravers, and sculptors. Whether it took the form of a skull, a skeleton, a tomb inscription, or a printed scroll, the *memento mori* was a favorite subject for artists in the medieval period and the Renaissance. A few brief examples may illustrate the nature of the genre and its effect upon the viewer.

A drawing by Albrecht Dürer, known variously as *The Pleasures of the World* and *Frolickers Threatened by Death* (1493/4, Oxford, Ashmolean Museum),[3] depicts a large number of persons strolling, eating, playing music and making love, none of them aware of the presence of Death in their midst. For the viewer, the effect is one of what might be called "pictorial irony," on the model of "dramatic irony"; he sees a menacing dimension to the situation that is apparently not shared by anyone within the picture frame.

Another Dürer work, an engraving of 1498 called *The Promenade*,[4] presents a stylishly dressed young couple strolling through an ideal landscape, enjoying the view and each other's company. In the middle distance to the right, however, lurking unseen behind a tree, is a skeletal figure of Death, grinning and holding above his head a fast-emptying hourglass. The young man's haunted expression suggests that he has seen or sensed the interloper, while his female companion remains oblivious to the threatening presence. The viewer, looking carefully, will discover the threat—but may not immediately realize that the grin (and the hourglass)

2. *Shakespeare's Living Art (Princeton, N.J., 1974), p. 11.*
3. Erwin Panofsky, *The Life and Art of Albrecht Dürer* (Princeton, N.J., 1955), plate 29.
4. *Ibid.*, plate 99. Cf. also Holbein's *Death and the New-Married Lady*, in Francis Douce, *Holbein's Dance of Death* (London, 1890), plate 29.

are also meant for him. In this case the viewer's response is, arguably, like Hamlet's double take—we comprehend two things in rapid succession, an image of earthly bliss (the lovers), and a sudden, undermining threat of death.

In Elizabethan portraiture the *memento mori* topos was of great importance; skulls, rotting cadavers, clocks, and watches frequently appeared as part of the composition—in effect moralizing on the time—emphasizing the transitoriness of the sitter and of his station in life.[5] The so-called Ashbourne portrait of Shakespeare, dated 1611, shows him with his arm supported by a skull, and numerous other portraits of the period depict the subject contemplating a skull, or resting his hand or foot upon one. Perhaps the most celebrated of such works is Holbein's painting *The Ambassadors* (1533), which shows us two opulently dressed young gentlemen surrounded by emblems of learning and power. The decorative pattern on the floor below them makes plain that the scene is Westminster Abbey, itself a seat of learning and power, but a curious design in that floor transforms the portrait into what is known as an anamorphism. Apparently an undifferentiated streak when the painting is viewed frontally, the design on the floor resolves itself into a skull when the spectator moves to the right edge of the painting. Earthly vanity and mortality occupy the same space and are, in essence, visual metaphors for one another. (It has been speculated that the skull may be, among other things, the artist's clever way of writing his signature, since his name, Holbein, means "hollow bone.")[6]

This kind of dualism or anamorphism is also known as perspective painting; the *OED* defines a perspective as "a picture or figure constructed so as to produce some fantastic effect—either appearing distorted or confused except from a particular point of view, or presenting totally different aspects from different points." *The Ambassadors* is clearly of the second type, and so presumably was a lost work by the Elizabethan miniaturist Nicholas Hilliard, recorded as "a cunning perspective of Death and a

5. See Roy C. Strong, *The English Icon* (New Haven, Conn., and London, 1969), pp. 37–40.

6. Ernest B. Gilman, *The Curious Perspective: Literary and Pictorial Wit in the Seventeenth Century* (New Haven, Conn., 1978), p. 103. Gilman's extended analysis of the portrait, pp. 98–104, is of considerable interest.

7. In the collection of Lord Lumley. Cited in Strong, *English Icon*, p. 39.

woman."[7] From its description this work would likewise have presented a visual metaphor or analogy, suggesting that although the woman possessed the outward shape of life (and perhaps beauty), Death lay beneath the surface, to be discovered by the onlooker as by the woman herself. If this was the case, the effect must have been very like that of Hamlet's speech in the graveyard as he held aloft Yorick's skull: "get you to my lady's chamber, and tell her, let her paint an inch thick, to this favor she must come" (V.i. 192–194).

There is, incidentally, much evidence in Shakespeare's plays that he was familiar with and fascinated by the phenomenon of the perspective painting. In a famous line from *Twelfth Night* the sudden appearance of the identical twins, Sebastian and Viola, is described as "a natural perspective, that is and is not!" (V.i.217). In *Richard II* Bushy likens the queen's grief at Richard's departure to "perspectives which, rightly gaz'd upon, / Show nothing but confusion; ey'd awry / Distinguish form" (II.ii.18–20). Cleopatra says ruefully of Antony that "Though he be painted one way like a Gorgon, / The other way's a Mars" (II.v.116–117). Interesting arguments can be—and have been—advanced for interpreting these plays themselves as larger perspectives.[8] For example, which is the hero of *Richard II*, Richard or Bolingbroke? Is the play Richard's tragedy, or the history of the young Henry IV? Or, along the same lines, is *Antony and Cleopatra* primarily a chronicle, or primarily a tragedy? Is the viewer's eye, at the last, upon the victory of Octavius or the glorious deaths of Antony and Cleopatra? But the particular perspective embodied in the twinning of life and death seems to me to be of special dramatic importance. It presents to the eye a visual emblem of the Christian paradox: we die to live. In the midst of life, Holbein's ambassadors are in death—or, as Shakespeare's imprisoned Claudio will put it in *Measure for Measure*, "To sue to live, I find I seek to die, / And seeking death, find life" (III.i.42–43).

Another popular artifact of the period was the so-called double-decker tomb, favored by persons of substance in Western Europe from the end of the fourteenth through the end of the sixteenth centuries.[9] Important English examples can be found in Lincoln, Canterbury, and Wells

8. For example, Norman Rabkin, "Rabbits, Ducks, and *Henry V*," *SQ*, XXVIII (1977), pp. 279–296, and Gilman, *Curious Perspective*, chaps. 4 and 5.

9. Erwin Panofsky, *Tomb Sculpture* (London, 1964), pp. 64–65.

cathedrals as well as in Arundel, Sussex. In these curious structures a lifelike effigy of the deceased, dressed in a costume befitting his exalted station in life, occupied what was in effect the upper berth of the tomb, while below in the lower berth appeared a deathly figure either covered with a shroud or—more usually—revealed as a skeletal cadaver in an advanced state of decomposition. Such skeletons were often graphically ornamented with toads and worms. The worldly figure was known— according to a contract of 1526—as a *representacion au vif*, and the cadaverous figure as a *representacion de la mort*; the juxtaposition of the two offered a pithy commentary on the enduring nature of human reputation and the leveling power of death. As the scroll in the gold casket of *The Merchant of Venice* will proclaim, "Gilded tombs do worms infold" (II.vii.69).

The *representacion de la mort*, also known as a *transi* figure, was (as its name implies) explicitly a *memento mori* and was often inscribed with appropriate sentiments: "I was what you are; you will be what I am," or, "Wretch, why are you proud? You are nothing more than ashes, and will, like me, be the food of worms." In just this way Shakespeare's Hotspur begins his own epitaph, "Percy, thou art dust, / And food for———," and Prince Hal completes his sentence, "for worms, brave Percy" (*1 Henry IV*, V.iv.85–87). The two parts of the tomb, like the two angles of the perspective painting, provide an interesting analogy to the problem of the literalized metaphor. Which is the metaphor—the *vanitas* grouping of ambassadors, or the skull unseen beneath their feet? Which is the literal fact—the stately effigy or the sculpted skeleton, the *representacion au vif* or the *representacion de la mort*? especially since somewhere about the tomb must be the actual remains of the dead. Tenor and vehicle become reciprocal here: handy-dandy, which is the literal, which is the figure? Or, to return to our example from *Hamlet*, what is the relationship between "My father, in his habit as he lived!" (III.iv.135), *au vif*, and the skulls and pocky corses of the graveyard, *de la mort*?

A related phenomenon with a similarly dramatic effect upon the viewer is that of the "shroud brasses" popular in England from the early fifteenth century to the end of the sixteenth. Most memorial brasses picture the deceased in the manner we have been calling *au vif*, dressed in clothing appropriate to his station in life: knight, bishop, titled lady. But these grisly and disquieting brasses, which reached their greatest popularity in Tudor times, instead present the subject wrapped in a shroud tied at head and foot, but open in the middle to reveal the breast and knees of the emaciated corpse. Sometimes, as with the double-decker tombs, the body is reduced to a skeleton; in other cases worms are shown devouring the corpse. In at least one instance the double focus of the tombs is also found in a brass: in a church in Lincolnshire the kneeling image of a knight in armor is engraved upon a small plate on the wall, while on the floor below the same knight is represented by a shrouded figure. [10] Frequently such brasses were installed during the lifetime of the subject, and were thus, once again, explicit reminders to him of his own mortality. In the seventeenth century John Donne theatrically recapitulated this practice as his own death approached. Commissioning the carving of a large wooden urn, he posed standing upon it for a "choice painter." As Izaak Walton tells us, he took "his winding-sheet in his hand, and, having put off all his clothes, had this sheet put upon him, and so tied with knots at his head and feet, and his hands so placed, as dead bodies are usually fitted to be shrouded and put into their coffin, or grave." When the picture was finished he had it set by his bedside where it "became his hourly object till his death." [11]

The skull was perhaps the most common of *memento mori* objects, appearing often in the form of a watch or other personal ornament; Mary Queen of Scots, for example, had a skull-shaped watch, and *memento mori* jewelry was worn by people in a wide variety of occupations and social positions, from procuresses, who wore death's-head rings on their middle fingers, to Martin Luther, whose ring reminded him, *"Mori saepe cogita."* [12] Frequently, as in this case, these ornaments spoke; that is, they

10. J. S. M. Ward, *Brasses* (Cambridge, Eng., 1912), pp. 81–82. See also Herbert W. Macklin, *Monumental Brasses* (London, 1890), p. 83.

11. Izaak Walton, "Life of Doctor John Donne," in *The Lives of Doctor John Donne, Sir Henry Walton, Mr. Richard Hooker, Mr. George Herbert* and *Doctor Herbert Sanderson* (London, 1895), pp. 47–48.

12. Kathleen Cohen, *Metamorphosis of a Death Symbol: The Transi Tomb in The Late Middle Ages and the Renaissance* (Berkeley, Calif., 1973), p. 85, n. 2; Theodore Spencer, *Death and Elizabethan Tragedy* (Cambridge, Mass., 1936), pp. 51–52, n. 36; and F. P. Weber, *Aspects of Death* (London, 1918), pp. 694, 722–724. The death's-head rings worn by bawds are mentioned in Marston's *The Dutch Courtesan*, ed. Peter Davison (Berkeley, Calif., 1968), I.ii.48–50: "As for their [bawds'] death, how can it bee bad, since their wickedness is always before their eyes, and a deathes head most commonly on their middle finger?"; in Massinger's *The Old Law, The Plays of Philip Massinger*, ed. W. Gifford (1813; rpt. New York, 1966), IV.i.181–184: "Sell some of thy clothes to buy thee a death's head, and put upon thy middle finger: your least considering bawd does so much"; and in Dekker's *Northward Ho, The Dramatic Works of Thomas Dekker*, ed. Fredson Bowers (Cambridge, Eng., 1955), IV.i.157–158: "As if I were a bawd, no ring pleases me but a deaths head."

bore inscriptions which voiced a suitable message, just as did the tombs. Thus Falstaff can admonish Doll Tearsheet, "Do not speak like a death's-head, do not bid me remember mine end" (*2 Henry IV*, II.iv.234–235), and the same intrepid Falstaff converts Bardolph's flaming red nose into a convenient symbol: "I make as good use of it [the nose] as many a man doth of a death's-head or a *memento mori*. I never see thy face but I think upon hell-fire and Dives that liv'd in purple; for there he is in his robes, burning, burning" (*1 Henry IV*, III.iii.29–33). Eloquent skulls are also to be found, among other places, in the *Et in Arcadia Ego* paintings of Guercino and Poussin. [13]

The conjunction of the skull and the jewel, the time bound and the timeless, was apparently a familiar figure of *vanitas;* we might consider Shakespeare's compelling use of it in *Richard III*, where the doomed Duke of Clarence dreams prophetically of his impending death. In his dream, he says, he saw

> Inestimable stones, unvalued jewels,
> All scatt'red in the bottom of the sea:
> Some lay in dead men's skulls, and in the holes
> Where eyes did once inhabit, there were crept,
> (As 'twere in scorn of eyes) reflecting gems,
> That woo'd the slimy bottom of the deep,
> And mock'd the dead bones that lay scatt'red by.
>
> (I.iv.27–33)

Notice "mock'd," and "as 'twere in scorn of eyes"; death is clearly the victor here. Much later in his career, Shakespeare would return to this image, but in a very different mood— in Ariel's second song in *The Tempest*: "Full fadom five thy father lies, / Of his bones are coral made: / Those are pearls that were his eyes" (I.ii.397–399). Here fear has been converted to wonder; Clarence's horror at decomposition and decay, so typical of the early Renaissance, becomes a sea change into something rich and

---

13. Erwin Panofsky, *"Et in Arcadia Ego*: Poussin and the Elegiac Tradition," in *Meaning in the Visual Arts* (Garden City, N.Y., 1955), pp. 295–320. (First published as *"Et in Arcadia Ego*: On the Conception of Transience in Poussin and Watteau," in *Philosophy and History, Essays Presented to Ernst Cassirer,* ed. R. Klibansky and H. J. Paton [Oxford, 1936], pp. 223–254.)

strange. And soon we learn that the father mourned here is not really dead. But this was at the close of Shakespeare's career, when perhaps for him, as for Prospero, every third thought would be his grave. The speaking skulls of earlier plays proclaim a very different message.

In the casket-choice scenes of *The Merchant of Venice*, the Prince of Morocco chooses the gold casket and finds within it a "carrion Death" (II.vii.63), a death's head or skull. The Prince of Arragon, choosing the silver casket, finds instead "the portrait of a blinking idiot" (II.ix.54), and quickly interprets the fool's head as his own. For both suitors the outcome is the same, a proscription against marriage and thus a symbolic death. The death's head and the fool's head, like the skull of Yorick, are in effect mirrors, showing those who gaze upon them the image of their own death. Ironically the third, or leaden, casket, with its threatening inscription ("Who chooseth me must give and hazard all he hath") *appears* to promise death—and Freud has made an interesting argument to this effect in his essay "The Theme of the Three Caskets." [14] But by reading the riddle correctly, and choosing the inevitability of death, Bassanio finds life, wealth, and Portia.

Perhaps the most extraordinary appearance of the skull as a *memento mori* in Renaissance drama occurs in III.v. of *The Revenger's Tragedy*, when Vindice dresses the skull of his fianceé in a headdress, wig, and veil, and poisons its lips to entrap the Duke who has seduced and murdered her. This scene is clearly indebted to the graveyard scene in *Hamlet*, as its language as well as its action makes plain. Hamlet's "Here hung those lips that I have kiss'd I know not how oft. Where be your gibes now?" (V.i.188–189) becomes Vindice's "A pretty hanging lip, that has forgot now to dissemble. / Methinks this mouth should make a swearer tremble" *Rev. Trag.* (III.v.56–57), [15] and "let her paint an inch thick, to this favor she must come" (*Hamlet*, V.i.193–194) becomes "Here's a cheek keeps her color let the wind go whistle" (*Rev. Trag.*, III.v.60). But Tourneur's revision rhetorically expands the economic concision of the graveyard scene in a remarkable way, The painted lady assumes a fuller identity as Vindice

14. First published in *Imago*, Bd. II., 1913; reprinted in *Character and Culture*, gen. ed. Philip Rieff, trans. C.J.M. Hubback (New York, 1963).

15. Cyril Tourneur, *The Revenger's Tragedy*, ed. Laurence J. Ross, Regents' Renaissance Drama Series (Lincoln, Nebr., 1966).

dwells with grisly self-indulgence on her ephemeral nature, employing as
he does so Hamlet's rhetorical strategy, a string of unanswered and un-
answerable questions.

> Does the silkworm expend her yellow labors
> For thee? For thee does she undo herself?
> Are lordships sold to maintain ladyships
> For the poor benefit of a bewitching minute?
> Why does yon fellow falsify highways . . .
>
> (III.v.71–75)

By 1607, when *The Revenger's Tragedy* was first performed, the business
with the skull in *Hamlet* would have been well known to playgoers, so that
this amplification, while typical of Tourneur's extravagance, might be
thought almost necessary, if the scene were to have a fresh and terrifying
impact. Thus while Yorick's skull is addressed by Hamlet for ten lines of
chilling prose, Vindice's "bony lady" becomes virtually the grotesque
equivalent of a ventriloquist's dummy, to whom and about whom he offers
more than sixty lines of grimly eloquent verse.

Only slightly less common than the skull as a favorite *memento mori*
object is the coffin or the emblematic corpse uncoffined. Marlowe had
provided such an emblematic stage prop in *Tamburlaine Part II,* in the
coffin of Tamburlaine's wife, Zenocrate, which is carried around—by his
order—wherever in the world Tamburlaine goes. "Till I die," he swears,
"thou shalt not be interr'd" (II.iv.132). [16] Despite this constant reminder,
however, Tamburlaine is surprised when the time does come for him to
die; despite its cumbersome omnipresence, that is, he does not understand
his own *memento mori.*

Characteristically, Shakespeare is more complex—and less heavy-
handed—in his elaboration on this theme. His onstage corpses are frequently treated, rather charmingly, with a wry—if macabre—sense of
humor. Falstaff on the battlefield at Shrewsbury stumbles upon the dead
body of Sir Walter Blunt, and comments with defensive irony: "Here's no
vanity! . . . I like not such grinning honor as Sir Walter hath. Give me

---

16. *The Complete Works of Chistopher Marlowe*, vol. I, ed. Fredson Bowers (Cambridge,
Eng., 1973).

life" (*1 Henry IV*, V.iii.33,58–59). The corpse, grimacing in death, becomes an instantly recognizable *memento mori*, and an ironic contrast to Falstaff's own feigned or figured death in the final scene.

At the beginning of *Richard III* the corpse of King Henry VI is borne in upon a hearse, mourned by the Lady Anne. "Poor key-cold figure of a holy king," she laments (I.ii.5)—and there enters to her immediately Henry's antithesis, the warm, unholy figure of Richard, bent on a mission of politic wooing. At his arrival she notes an alarming phenomenon; the dead king's wounds begin to "bleed afresh," a deluge most unnatural," she says, "from cold and empty veins where no blood dwells" (ll. 55–61). Angrily Anne accuses Richard of being the "inhuman" cause of both the death and the unnatural blood, but nonetheless she remains onstage to talk with him for almost 200 lines, while the coffin lies, in eloquent silence, center stage. When she finally takes her leave, Richard's ring is on her finger and the corpse of King Henry is in Richard's hands. I have seen productions of the play in which, despite the textual suggestion that the body is open to view, a closed coffin has been used, and the odd pair of "lovers," Richard and Anne, sat upon it most familiarly while they talked. In any case, the onstage presence of the body throughout this long and peculiar wooing scene underscores the elements of unnaturalism and of Richard's tour de force, wooing the lady in the presence of her father-in-law's corpse. The body itself is yet another ironic *memento mori*, a literalization of Richard's lines on Anne's departure: "Was ever woman in this human woo'd? Was ever woman in this humor won?" At the same time the coffin is a palpable intimation of the truth of his next line, "I'll have her, but I will not keep her long" (I.ii.227–229).

We might compare this scene in terms of its stage picture to the Queen's closet scene in *Hamlet*, where the body of the slain Polonius also lies recumbent on the stage for some 200 lines before Hamlet decides to "lug the guts into the neighbor room" (III.iv.212). In both scenes a man and woman discourse about love and murder, seemingly oblivious to the dead body at their feet; in each the dead man is briefly lamented, then ignored, but his presence on the stage frames and deepens the audience's understanding, like the little grinning Death of the Dürer engraving. Moreover, in the closet scene there are not one but two versions of *memento mori*: the "foolish prating knave" who "is now most still, most secret, and most grave" (ll. 214–215), and the speaking shade of Old Hamlet, visible and audible to Hamlet and the audience, but unperceived by the bewildered Gertrude. "Do you see nothing there?" asks the son, and the mother replies, "Nothing at all, yet all that is I see," "Nor did you nothing hear?" "No, nothing but ourselves" (ll. 131–134). Like Dürer's doomed maiden, she is oblivious to the proximity of death. The Ghost's "visitation" is, as he points out, explicitly a reminder, and his admonition, "Do not forget!" (l. 110), is another version of "remember me." The scene as a whole thus works on several levels at once to remind the audience, as well as Hamlet, that in the midst of life we are in death.

The coffin of the slain Richard II becomes a similarly effective *memento mori* at the close of the play that bears his name. In Act V, scene 4, Sir Pierce Exton muses on words he claims to have heard twice from the new king, Henry IV: "Have I no friend will rid me of this living fear?" (l. 2). Expecting a reward, Exton sets out to kill Richard. In the meantime, Henry has been trying to bring civil strife to a close, rewarding his supporters, beheading the Oxford traitors, but in a gesture of mercy pardoning his old enemy the Bishop of Carlisle. However, when in the final scene Exton enters to him with the body, all Henry's careful plans are undone. As a theatrical event, the entry of the coffin will be monumental and stately, as several men move slowly forward under their burden of death. And now again we have a moment of dramatic reification, as Exton transmutes Henry's phrase "living fear" to something both more concrete and more ambiguous. "Great King," he says, "within this coffin I present / Thy buried fear" (V.vi.30–31). Exton's intended meaning is clear: that which was once living is now buried; that which was once feared need no longer be so. But Henry's "buried fear" is something else: a secret, unrevealed fear, a fear of guilt and blood upon his hands, the fear that he will fail in his attempt to reunite and preserve the kingdom. The physical manifestation of the coffin on the stage unburies the buried fear and makes it live. Once again, a process of unmetaphoring and remetaphoring reifies dramatic action and throws across both stage and play the long black shadow of death.

The most interesting uses of *memento mori* in drama, however, are not such literal references to skulls and skeletons, coffins and cadavers but rather those characters and scenes which seem to embody the spirit and something of the dramatic impact of this topos in the context of a play's design. It is interesting to note that Death as a dramatic character makes very few personal appearances upon the English stage. In the N Town play *The Death of Herod* a figure called *Mors* enters, clad in rags and covered with worms, to claim the king's soul, announcing, "I am Deth, Goddys masangere," (l. 177)," [17] and in *Everyman* Death again appears as a "mighty messengere" from God (l. 63). Much later, in Shakespeare's time, Death once more treads the boards in a kind of cameo role as part of the chorus to Kyd's play *Soliman and Perseda*, where he is accompanied by Love and Fortune. [18] But despite the cartloads of bodies that lay strewn across the stage at the close of Elizabethan tragedies, the literal figure of Death seems to have appeared very infrequently in the history of English drama. And that is probably as it should be. "O, death's a great disguiser," says the Duke in *Measure for Measure* (IV.ii.174), and the dramatic impact of a confrontation with Death is much increased if we do not at first recognize him for who—or what—he is. In effect, the actor, the reader, the spectator, all become interpreters, trying to descry Death before he puts his hand on our shoulders. "This fell sergeant, Death, / Is strict in his arrest," says Hamlet (V.ii.336–337)—and all the more so if we do not see him coming. The shock of recognition is itself a part of growth, a step toward self-knowledge—the readiness is all. And the presence of a disguised Death, at once psychologically persuasive and theatrically effective, is central to the design of Shakespearean drama.

One striking example of a disguised but personated Death from the works of one of Shakespeare's contemporaries is that of the Mower in Marlowe's *Edward II*. The characters in Marlowe's play are entirely historical and realistic—with names like Gaveston, Mortimer, Spencer, and so on—until the end of Act IV, when the wretched Edward, believing himself to have escaped his enemies and found refuge among a contemplative order of monks, receives three unexpected visitors. The stage direction reads, "*Enter with Welsh hooks*, Rice ap Howell, *a* Mower, *and the Earle of*

---

17. *Medieval Drama*, ed. David Bevington (Boston, 1975). Death's costume is described in ll. 272–273.

18. *The Works of Thomas Kyd*, ed. Frederic S. Boas (1901; rpt. Oxford, 1955).

Leicester." The Mower has been characterized a few lines earlier as "a gloomie fellow in a meade belowe" (IV.vi.29)[19] who "gave a long looke after" (l. 30) Edward and his party as they passed in secrecy. When the three figures enter it is he who points to the king, saying, "those be the men ye seeke" (l. 46). His only other line, spoken after Edward has been borne away to the place that will be his death, is highly suggestive in the dramatic context. He wants to be paid, and so he addresses Rice ap Howell, his employer: "Your worship, I trust, will remember me?" "Remember thee, fellow?" is the reply. "What else? Follow me to the towne" (IV.vi.117–118). Here the conjunction of the Mower, the Welsh hook (a curved blade attached to a handle), and the injunction to "Remember me" strongly suggest the presence of a *memento mori* figure, and this identification is made more persuasive by the abstraction of his name ("Mower"), the traditional iconographic associations of the mower's role, and the fact that he appears only—and startlingly—in this one scene. Indeed, the only way the spectators could know he *was* a mower—since he is never directly addressed as such—is by the fact that he carried a scythe. Even Marlowe's descriptive characterization supports the sense of symbolism here, for a "gloomie" mower is very like a grim reaper.

Less archetypal than the Mower but equally remarkable in dramatic effect is a figure who appears at the end of Shakespeare's *Troilus and Cressida*, just before Hector meets his death at the hands of Achilles and the Myrmidons. Here the stage direction reads simply, *"Enter one in armor."* Following a chivalric tradition, Hector covets the sumptuous armor as a battle prize and challenges the newcomer to fight. The "one" never speaks; he appears in Act V, scene 6, then the two figures battle offstage, and in Act V, scene 8, we again see Hector, now disarming himself, as he stands over the slain body of the "one in armor." Hector's words in this scene are particularly evocative: "Most putrefied core, so fair without, / Thy goodly armor thus hath cost thy life" (V.viii.1–2). (We might notice here the parallel to the double-decker tomb: putrefaction juxtaposed to earthly splendor.) Part of the effect of these two scenes is their contrast with the scene that comes between them, V.vii. In that

19. *The Complete Works of Christopher Marlowe,* vol. II, ed. Fredson Bowers (Cambridge, Eng., 1973).

scene Achilles tells the Myrmidons to surround Hector and kill him in the "fellest"—that is, the foulest—manner, and Thersites refuses to fight the bastard Margarelon. Thus mercenaries (the Myrmidons) and a coward (Thersites) are juxtaposed to Hector the honorable warrior, and demonstrate the futility of his solitary struggle for civic pride and personal glory. But the putrefied core seems to reify, to personify, not only the hollow victory of war but also the shadow of death—Hector's death. The weary Hector, unarmed, is easy prey for Achilles and his men. Again the silence of the figure emphasizes both his menace and his symbolic status. Appearing—like the Mower—on the eve of death, he seems to come, like him, from another dramatic world.

A somewhat different but related figure who appears near a play's close is the apothecary in *Romeo and Juliet*. As described by Romeo, he seems the apotheosis of Death himself: "meagre were his looks, / Sharp misery had worn him to the bones," Romeo remembers (V.i.40–41), and, face to face with him, he observes, "Famine is in thy cheeks, / Need and oppression starveth in thy eyes" (ll. 69–70). Two short scenes later, in Juliet's tomb, Romeo will refer to a personified Death directly as a "lean abhorred monster" (V.iii.104), a traditional picture but one which inevitably recalls the apothecary. I think that this episode is to some slight extent undercut by its own explicitness. Romeo has come to the shop for poison with which to kill himself, and he moralizes on the exchange in a familiar fashion: "There is thy gold, worse poison to men's souls, / Doing more murther in this loathsome world, / Than these poor compounds that thou mayest not sell. / I sell thee poison, thou hast sold me none" (V.i.80–83). The equivalence of death and gold is proverbial, but in traditional folklore Death usually entraps his victims only after they fail a test of civility, disinterestedness, or lack of greed; thus the old man in the *Pardoner's Tale* only points the way to the fatal tree after he has been abused and insulted by the three rioters. Shakespeare's apothecary is a variation on this theme; his reluctance stems from timidity and fear of the law, rather than from cunning or insult. As a result the death of Romeo comes not as a surprise, but as a disquieting expectation. He seeks out Death, knowing exactly— or thinking he knows exactly—what he is doing. The final irony lies not, as in folklore, in the demise of the young quester, but instead in the fact—already painfully known to the audience—that this quest for death is based on a false premise, since Juliet still lives. Although the source of the irony changes, the irony itself remains. The "true apothecary" is, as so often in Shakespeare, a "false seems true" (*Measure for Measure,* V.i.67).

It is interesting to note that these deathly figures do not appear only in the tragedies and histories; in fact, a great number can be found in Shakespeare's comedies, perhaps because in the comedies no character who appears onstage actually suffers death by the play's end. We hear of deaths, but we do not see them—nobody we meet dies. But the threat of death, bounding the play, gives it dimension and meaning, a reason for the end to the revels. The bound Egeon of *The Comedy of Errors* is such a figure, framing the play with a visual emblem of mortality in its first and last scenes. If he is not ransomed before sundown he will die, and the farcical action of the main plot must compete with the audience's memory of his plight. In a recent production of the play in Berkeley, California, Egeon's lengthy opening monologue (often a trial for directors) was accompanied by the actions of a hangman on the upper stage, who prepared his noose as the bound man spoke. [20] The noose as well as the prisoner provided—once again—a kind of *memento mori*, hanging over the ensuing developments in the plot and incorporating the many comic references to "rope's ends" into a darker design. In this case an imaginative act of staging helped to bring out a meaning implicit in the play.

Usually such meanings are built-in, so to speak, by the playwright and provide for that dramatic shock of recognition which is the essence of the stage *memento mori*. Thus at the close of *Love's Labor's Lost* we see a stage crowded with brightly costumed figures—the "Nine Worthies" in their togas and swords, the lords and ladies in elegant court dress—when the messenger Marcade enters with news of the death of the King of France. The Princess immediately guesses his message, and we may reasonably conjecture that one reason she does so is that he is dressed in the stark blackness of mourning. The contrast between his clothing and that of the others creates on the stage a strikingly visible *memento mori*. Like other such figures, Marcade is almost silent, his news communicated by his presence as much as his words. "The King your father,—" he begins. "Dead, for

---

20. A production of the Berkeley Shakespeare Festival, 1978, directed by Julian Lopez-Morillas. As reported by Laurence H. Jacobs, *SQ,* XXX (1979), 249.

my life!" interjects the Princess, and he replies only, "Even so: my tale is told" (V.ii.719–720). The sudden intrusion of silence and death into a play so otherwise wordy and playful is dramatically startling. But we should bear in mind the fact that the opening lines of *Love's Labor's Lost* are the King of Navarre's vainglorious speculations upon his own epitaph. "Let fame, that all hunt after in their lives, / Live regist'red upon our brazen tombs, / And then grace us in the disgrace of death" (I.i.1–3). What began as play-acting becomes harshly real; the imagined tomb is transmuted into the physical sign of death. The subject—though hidden—has always been present.

Yet another telling visual metaphor is provided by Claudio in *Measure for Measure*, who, like so many of these figures, appears in an emblematic guise near the end of the play. Sentenced to die, indeed believed to be dead by all but the Duke, the Provost, and the audience, he appears in the final scene "muffled"—that is, in a symbolic face-covering shroud. Moreover, he does not speak, even after his identity is revealed. Costume, silence, and dramatic context once again underscore the medial position of the character, suspended between life and death. Claudio himself has already confronted the inevitability of death, in a striking eschatological passage (III.i.117–131). Indeed, the very fact that he has become, in the Duke's phrase, "absolute for death" (III.i.5) is what makes him eligible to perform this new dramatic function. As the guilty Angelo admits his errors and stands condemned for the supposed execution of Claudio, Claudio appears before him in disguise, as something both more and less than a dramatic character. Visually as well as morally, he provides a mirror and a *memento mori* for Angelo, who now himself becomes absolute for death and seeks only to die. The Arden editor, J. W. Lever, speculates that the muffled Claudio may represent "blind love," [21] but he seems to me at least equally close to the biblical figure of Lazarus, who came forth from his grave "bound hand and foot with graveclothes; and his face was bound about with a napkin" (John 11:44). Lazarus, like Claudio, is restored to a loving sister who has put her faith in a powerful Lord.

Restorations similar to Claudio's occur at the end of several other Shakespearean plays, and they too incorporate the familiar but effective

---

21. *Measure for Measure* (London, 1965), p. 147 n.

devices of silence, disguise, and riddle or enigma. In *Much Ado About Nothing* the peevish Count Claudio thinks he has killed Hero by slandering her in public; in the final scene she appears mysteriously masked, addresses him in riddling language ("And when I liv'd, I was your other wife" [V.iv.60]), and reveals herself when he has shown repentance and faith. In *All's Well That Ends Well* the churlish Bertram is suspected of "foully snatch[ing]" (V.iii.154) the life of Helena, whom he married under duress, and who is now thought dead; he too shows a change of heart and is rewarded by Helena's reappearance, again heralded by an appropriately symbolic riddle: "one that's dead is quick" (V.iii.303). The ultimate refinement of this topos, of course, comes in *The Winter's Tale,* where the slandered queen, Hermione, also thought to be dead, appears onstage in the guise of a funeral effigy—a statue—a literal *memento mori*. Her unworthy husband, Leontes, has paid penance by visiting what he takes to be her gravesite daily for sixteen years; in the play's climactic scene the "statue" comes to life before the astonished eyes of Leontes, his newfound daughter, and the audience in the theater—which has not in this case previously been let in on the secret. The suppression of that information (that Hermione is alive), and the remarkable stage action of the statue's awakening provide for what is surely the crowning instance of metaphoring and unmetaphoring in any of Shakespeare's plays. But in each of these cases—in *Much Ado, All's Well*, and *The Winter's Tale*—an explicit period of mourning precedes the restoration. The erring husband or suitor—and with him, the audience—is made to meditate on mortality and the pain of loss.

A more complex *memento mori* pattern occurs in *Twelfth Night*, to some eyes one of the most festive of Shakespeare's comedies. The play opens with an account of Olivia's obsessive mourning: for seven years

> like a cloistress she will veiled walk,
> And water once a day her chamber round
> With eye-offending brine; all this to season
> A brother's dead love
>
> (I.i.27–30)

Notice the word "season" here—to cure, to preserve her mourning; notice also the word order—"a brother's dead love," not "a dead brother's love."

This is the quintessence of the morbid and the self-absorbed; Olivia's brother's death has, imaginatively, become her own. The chamber in which she paces is an enclosed space symbolic at once of her virginity and of the tomb, both prisons she voluntarily chooses; she is her own repressive parent. The veil she wears, like Claudio's muffle and Hero's mask, is an outward sign of inward death.

In a sense this "death" is retrieved or reversed by the circumstances of her marriage to Sebastian, who enters the wedding scene exulting, "This is the air, that is the glorious sun" (IV.iii. 1)—a clear reversal of Olivia's airless self-cloistering. Moreover, their marriage is to be performed in a nearby chantry—and a chantry was not merely a chapel, but a place specifically established for the perpetual chanting of prayers for the dead. Like the double-decker tomb, this was a favorite memorial practice in medieval and Tudor England; both Henry V and Henry VIII built elaborate chantries for themselves in Westminster Abbey, and no fewer than six bishops established chantries in Winchester Cathedral alone in the period from 1345 to 1555. [22] If, as seems likely, Olivia's chantry is a family endowment, her marriage is to be performed in the same place where her brother's death is mourned, one ceremony complements and completes the other.

But there is a third locale in *Twelfth Night* which is directly analogous to the chamber and the chantry: the dark room or "house" to which Malvolio is taken to cure his supposed madness. An interesting linguistic clue unites these places and provides a pattern which may, I think, be worthy of our notice. When the false letter is laid in his path, Malvolio finds no difficulty in interpreting it as a declaration of Olivia's love for himself. "Why, this is evident to any formal capacity. There is no obstruction in this" (II.v. 116–118). He then, as bidden in the letter, presents himself to Olivia in yellow stockings, cross-gartered, and smiling. Why does he smile, Olivia asks. "I sent for thee upon a sad occasion." And Malvolio replies, "Sad, lady? I could be sad. This does make some obstruction in the blood, this cross-gartering, but what of that?" (III.iv. 18–22). "Some obstruction in the blood." Finally, when at Toby's suggestion he is taken to the dark room and bound, Malvolio is visited by the Fool, in the guise

22. T.S.R. Boase, *Death in the Middle Ages* (New York, 1972), pp. 62–73.

of Sir Topas, and in nonsense terms the Fool tries to persuade him that the place is full of light. "Why, it hath bay windows transparent as barricadoes, and the clerestories toward the south north are as lustrous as ebony; and yet complainest thou of obstruction?" (IV.ii.36–39). Notice, "obstruction" again.

Clearly Malvolio is obstructed or repressed in a Freudian sense. But the word "obstruction" is interesting here in another sense as well, for Shakespeare uses it only twice more in his plays, and in each case the reference is clearly to the condition of death. In the second part of *Henry IV* the Archbishop of York, noting the sickness in the state, speaks of the necessity to "purge th' obstructions which begin to stop / Our very veins of life" (IV.i.65–66). More strikingly, Claudio in *Measure for Measure*, in his own imaginative confrontation with death, uses the proverbial phrase "cold obstruction" to mean death. "Ay, but to die, and go we know not where, / To lie in cold obstruction and to rot; / This sensible warm motion to become / A kneaded clod" (III.i.117–120).[23] Malvolio's obstruction is likewise a kind of death. His incarceration is another un-metaphoring or literalization, since he has *always* been in one sense in a dark room and bound—and bound, as the cross-gartering demonstrates, by his own obstructive attitudes and actions. Maria's letter and its drama-tic consequences, then, reveal—once again, by unmetaphoring and remetaphoring—an essential truth about Malvolio's psychological condi-tion. At the same time they enforce the parallel between Malvolio and Olivia, both sick of self-love, abnormally sad and mournful, confined to dark prisons of their own devising.

Now to say this, I should point out, is really to say no more than what many readers and audiences already sense about Malvolio. "Sad and civil," an enemy to song and revelry, puritanical in the extreme, he personates a deathly spirit in Olivia's household and is fittingly chosen to rule that household during her period of self-indulgent mourning. Malvolio's first words in the play concern "infirmity" and the "pangs of death" (I.v.75–76), and he is almost certainly dressed in black; as John Russell Brown observes, in his proposal for an ideal production of the play, "Olivia

23. Such passages of direct imaginative confrontation with death are fairly rare in Shakespeare, but compare Juliet as she is about to take the Friar's potion (*R&J*, IV.ii.32–54).

would, of course, wear black while in mourning, and Malvolio always—the only character to take no colour from the sun."[24]

It is useful to compare Malvolio to another figure from the comedies who is likewise traditionally dressed in black—the "melancholy Jaques" in *As You Like It*. His melancholy is really a kind of narcissistic self-absorption, not as dangerous or malevolent as Malvolio's, but equally unfit for inclusion in the play's festive close. For Jaques *memento mori* is a posture, a role, a fashionable game. His "All the world's a stage" speech pictures the seventh age of second childishness as "sans teeth, sans eyes, sans taste, sans every thing" (II.vii. 166) and is immediately undercut by the arrival onstage of the loyal old Adam, the opposite in all ways to this gloomy picture of decay. But the most straightforward expression of *memento mori* sentiments in *As You Like It* comes to us through what is in effect a human mirror. Jaques, wandering in the forest, has met a fool who ostentatiously "drew a dial from his poke" (II.vii.20) and "moral[led] on the time" (l. 29). The fool, of course, is Touchstone, and what he has really been doing is mocking Jaques's own attitudinizing: "And so from hour to hour, we ripe and ripe, / And then from hour to hour, we rot and rot; / And thereby hangs a tale" (ll. 26–28). No wonder Jaques is delighted: what he is admiring is a mirror of himself. "A motley fool. A miserable world!" (l. 13), he cries—taking as much pleasure in the one as in the other. "I am ambitious for a motley coat" (l. 43). Moreover, this playful proposal to exchange black coat for motley coat, like Touchstone's playful expression of *memento mori* ideas, has a further significance here, because from the medieval period on Death was often portrayed in the livery of a fool.

This tradition stems in part from the Dance of Death, an artistic convention immensely popular in the fifteenth century and after, in which dancing, grinning skeletons were seen to lead away emperor and pope, peasant and king.[25] We know that a painting on this theme was displayed in Shakespeare's church at Stratford-on-Avon.[26] In Holbein's popular woodcut series on the Dance of Death, there is a plate depicting Death and

---

24. John Russell Brown, *Shakespeare's Plays in Performance* (London, 1969), p. 234.

25. See Austin Dobson, ed., *The Dance of Death* (London, 1892); James Midgley Clark, *The Dance of Death in the Middle Ages and the Renaissance* (Glasgow, 1950); and L. P. Kurtz, *The Dance of Death and the Macabre Spirit in European Literature* (New York, 1934).

26. Douce, *Holbein's Dance of Death,* p. 46.

the Queen, in which Death is shown in full fool's costume, complete with cap and bells. [27] Verbal references to Death as a fool occur frequently in Shakespeare's plays; Richard II in a famous passage muses that "within the hollow crown / That rounds the mortal temples of a king / Keeps Death his court, and there the antic sits . . . " (III.ii.160–162), and when old Talbot is confronted with the dead body of his son in the first part of *Henry VI* he cries out angrily against "Thou antic Death, which laugh'st us here to scorn" (IV.vii.18). I mentioned earlier that in *The Merchant of Venice* the fool's head in the silver casket becomes symbolically parallel to the death's head in the gold one. In *As You Like It* the fool mocks Jaques's *memento mori* notions—and the audience is reminded of them. In a sense death is a touchstone here, giving dimension and value to all the events of the play. In *Twelfth Night* the fool, whose name means feasting, the opposite of death, sings songs that address the subject of death directly: "Come away death," he sings, and "Youth's a stuff will not endure," and "The rain it raineth every day." Like Touchstone, Feste is not a bringer of death, but he is a constant reminder of it. And this contiguity of death and folly underscores the truth-telling function allowed to the traditional fool. He alone can mention the unmentionable—and what is more unmentionable, what is more unthinkable, than the fact of one's own death? Thus when in *Hamlet* the prince abandons his "inky cloak" for his "antic disposition," he is really only exchanging one *memento mori* for another. Playing the fool—as well as the madman—he brings Gertrude and the Claudius court to a belated recognition of the meaning of death—and its imminence. Hamlet in his mother's bedchamber, wearing his antic disposition, is in a way a dramatized version of Holbein's woodcut: Death and the Queen.

"Death's a great disguiser"—or, to borrow a phrase from *Henry V*, "Your Majesty came not like yourself" (IV.viii.50). Although he is listed in no Shakespearean cast of characters, in play after play Death makes a dramatic entrance. He is rather like that extra devil who, it is said, occasionally appeared onstage in productions of *Doctor Faustus*—and who may have been the reason why Edward Alleyn wore "a surplis, / With a

27. *Ibid.*, plate 11.

crosse vpon his breast" [28] whenever he played the part. To recognize the interloper who is always present is the task at once of audience and actor ("Do you see nothing there?" "Nothing at all; yet all that is I see"). Pericles, in the court of Antiochus, gazes on the impaled heads of previous suitors, and addresses his perfidious host: "Antiochus, I thank thee, who hath taught / My frail mortality to know itself . . . For death remembered should be like a mirror" (I.i.41–45). Here we have come full circle from the point where we began. And were we now to look once more upon the graveyard scene in *Hamlet*, we might find that it bore a curious resemblance to an engraving by the great sixteenth-century anatomist, Vesalius. In that engraving—as, symbolically, in many of Shakespeare's plays—the figure that leans upon a tomb, and meditates upon a skull, is itself a skeleton. [29]

28. S. Rowlands, *The Knave of Clubs* (London, 1609), p. 29. Cited in *Doctor Faustus*, ed. John D. Jump (London, 1962), p. lviii.

29. First published in 1543, and widely reprinted in Shakespeare's time. Roland Mushat Frye was the first to bring this witty and evocative engraving to my attention, initially in a talk at the Shakespeare Association of America annual meeting (1978), then in the published version of that talk, "Ladies, Gentlemen, and Skulls: *Hamlet* and the Iconographic Tradition," *SQ*, XXX (1979), 15–28.

Elizabethan Dramatic Conventions and Elizabethan Reality

ROBERT R. HELLENGA

M ANY OF THE INTERPRETATIVE CRUXES of Elizabethan drama arise from a discrepancy between what characters *are* and what they *do*. One-dimensional characters—humorous types and stock characters—present no difficulties because they more or less are what they do. More fully realized figures, however, frequently disturb us by what Madeleine Doran has called 'a disconcerting unpredictability that sometimes militates against a coherent total impression, whether of type or individual." [1] The difficulty is most acute in Shakespeare, whose characters, of course, are the most fully realized in Elizabethan drama.

The traditional ways of accounting for this discrepancy do not reinforce each other. The first explains away problematic behavior, such as Hamlet's delay, or Othello's credulity, or Helena's means of consummating her marriage in *All's Well That Ends Well*, by appealing to dramatic conventions which obviate the need for adequate and consistent motivation even in "realistic" characters. "The difficulty in Shakespeare's case," says Muriel Bradbrook, "arises from the difference between the realism with which he presents his characters and the conventional manner in which he motivates them. Leontes is perhaps the most striking example." [2] The second appeals to depth psychology. Inconsistencies which on the surface appear to be unrealistic, because they cannot be accounted for by rationalistic notions of

1. Madeleine Doran, *Endeavors of Art: A Study of Form in Elizabethan Drama* (Madison, Wis., 1954), p. 217.

the psyche, can be explained by the insights of modern depth psychology. Even Leontes is susceptible to analysis: he conforms to "a typical paranoiac pattern" by projecting onto Hermione his own unconscious homosexual attraction for Polixenes. [3] And it is important to realize that the case of Leontes, though extreme, is not essentially different from the more subtle and perplexing problems we encounter in the great tragedies.

The controversy over Othello's credulity illustrates the dilemma more fully. What is it, asks Professor E. E. Stoll, that makes a generous and unsuspicious hero believe a person "whom he does not love or really know and has no right reason to trust, to the point of disbelieving persons whom he loves and has every reason to trust . . . without proof of the accuser's or inquiry and investigation of his own"? It is, say critics of the first school, "the convention of the culumniator credited." [4] As in all great stories, "probability or psychological reasonableness" is a "secondary consideration":

Their improbability is the price of their effectiveness: such fine and fruitful situations life itself does not afford. The sharper conflict provokes the bigger passion; the more striking contrast produces the bigger effect: and to genius the improbability is only a challenge. [5]

Psychological explanations are dismissed as "elaborate," "ill-founded," irrelevant to literature.

Needless to say, this has not discouraged psychologically oriented critics from seeking other solutions to the problem, and Othello's behavior has been attributed, in Jungian terms, to the surfacing of his *shadow* "in the shape of 'honest Iago,'" which so overwhelms him that his *anima* (projected on Desdemona) assumes the "antinomial quality of a witch" who

2. Muriel C. Bradbrook, *Themes and Conventions of Elizabethan Tragedy* (Cambridge, Eng., 1966), pp. 63–64.

3. J.I.M. Stewart, *Character and Motive in Shakespeare* (London, 1949), p. 35. Cf. C. L. Barber, "'Thou That Beget'st Him That Did Thee Beget': Transformation in 'Pericles' and 'The Winter's Tale,'" *ShS*, XXII (1969), 66.

4. E. E. Stoll, *Art and Artifice in Shakespeare: A Study in Dramatic Contrast and Illusion* (Cambridge, Eng., 1933). The quotation is from p. 7. The convention is named in the Table of Contents, p. vii. Cf. Bradbrook, p. 63.

must be destroyed. [6] In Freudian terms Othello appears as "a man wrapped in self-delusion, of a known psychological type in which overtrust speedily shifts to undertrust on the first provocation, loving not a real woman but an image of his own creating . . . a man eaten out by 'a habit of approving self-dramatisation.' " [7]

Does the action, then, turn on a well-worn convention which obviates the need for tedious exposition and consistency of character, or has Shakespeare made "a plunge for the collective unconscious"? [8] A number of half-hearted attempts have been made to resolve this dilemma and others like it by bringing a knowledge of Elizabethan psychology to bear upon Elizabethan dramatic characters. In Elizabethan psychological theory, for example, the "passions" tended to be regarded as something external; they come upon a man from outside and are not necessarily connected with his character or "ethos." Othello, for example, was a man "not easily jealous, but, being wrought, perplexed in the extreme"; his jealous passion, that is, is not connected with his character. Even the most persuasive of these accounts, however, such as Madeleine Doran's, which I have been paraphrasing, [9] are open to a fatal objection which has been raised by numerous critics: did Shakespeare imitate life or did he imitate Elizabethan theories about life? Presumably he imitated life itself, in which case we should expect modern psychology to provide a more adequate interpretative framework for *Othello* than the Elizabethan faculty psychology; and we should expect Freud's *Interpretation of Dreams* to throw more light on *Hamlet* than Timothy Bright's *Treatise of Melancholy* (London, 1586). [10]

5. Stoll, p. 2.

6. Sitansu Maitra, *Psychological Realism and Archetypes: The Trickster in Shakespeare* (Calcutta, 1967), pp. 75, 76.

7. This is J.I.M. Stewart's conflation of Othello as perceived by T. S. Eliot, L. Kirschbaum, and F. R. Leavis (pp. 104–105). Stewart's own interpretation is even more ingenious.

8. Maitra, p. 76.

9. *Endeavors of Art*, pp. 234–238.

10. For further discussion of this issue see Paul Gottschalk, *The Meanings of "Hamlet": Modes of Literary Interpretation Since Bradley* (Albuquerque, N.M., 1972), chap. 3; and J. Leeds Barroll, "Psychology and Psychiatry in Renaissance England," chap. 1 of *Artificial Persons: The Formation of Character in the Tragedies of Shakespeare* (Columbia, S.C., 1974).

Freud introduces the subject of Hamlet's Oedipus complex in section V.b, b. of *The Interpretation of Dreams*, trans. James Strachey (New York, n.d. [1955]), pp. 264–266.

The question of whether Hamlet's melancholy is "natural" or "adust" will never hold the attention of more than a handful of specialists unless it can be demonstrated that Elizabethan psychology provides us with a good account of reality itself and not simply "a crude explanation of observable facts, based on the science of the Middle Ages and motivated in its development by a desire to understand the functioning of the soul for the better regulation of conduct." [11] No such reconsideration of Elizabethan psychological theory is on the immediate horizon; but, as I have indicated, the advent of historical psychology—the recognition, that is, that the discipline of psychology is not ahistorical—encourages us to entertain the possibility that Elizabethan literary figures reflect differences between the Elizabethan age and our own which are experiential and not merely conceptual.

We can, I think, arrive at a more satisfactory rapprochement between "conventional" and "psychological" approaches to problems of this sort by reconsidering the orthodox assumption, shared by such distinguished critics as Muriel Bradbrook, Una Ellis-Fermor, E. E. Stoll, John Dover Wilson, and, more recently, Raymond Williams and Alan Dessen, that Elizabethan dramatic conventions were in essence convenient shortcuts— more or less arbitrary agreements between dramatists and audiences, concluded for the sake of dramatic utility. [12] It is surprising that this view has not been challenged, for we have come to recognize that literary conventions are central, not peripheral, to the reality of literature. We acknowledge, for example, that Donne's conceits and Pope's couplets were essential to their respective visions of the world, not arbitrary devices which they found convenient; but we persist in treating Elizabethan dramatic

11. Ruth Anderson, *Elizabethan Psychology and Shakespeare's Plays*, University of Iowa Humanistic Studies, vol. III, no. 4 (Iowa City, 1927), p. 154.

12. This is essentially the view put forward by William Archer in his famous attack on Elizabethan drama (*The Old Drama and the New* [Boston, 1923]). Modern critics do not share Archer's hostility, but they have not revised his basic assumptions about the function of dramatic conventions. See, for particulars, Bradbrook, p. 4; Una Ellis-Fermor, *The Jacobean Drama: An Interpretation* (London, 1936; rev. ed., 1958), pp. 49–50; Stoll, pp. 79, 3; John Dover Wilson, *What Happens in "Hamlet"* (New York, 1935), pp. 219–220, 229; Raymond Williams, *Drama from Ibsen to Brecht*, 2d ed. (London, 1968), pp. 12–16; Alan C. Dessen, "Elizabethan Audiences and the Open Stage: Recovering Lost Conventions," *The Yearbook of English Studies*, X (1980), 1–20.

conventions as useful shortcuts which audiences were willing to put up with in exchange for concentration, intensity, and special effects. The reason for this, no doubt, is that we find the Elizabethan conventions harder to accommodate to our own sense of reality than conceits and heroic couplets. But this indicates something about our own sense of reality as well as about bed tricks and the like; for we must remember that conventions do not ordinarily appear "conventional"—that is, unrealistic—to those who are sufficiently close to them. Literary historians, even without an adequate theory of change, have shown that the advent of a new set of conventions, such as the courtly love conventions, or stream of consciousness, is a matter of substantive change in our perception of reality; and new conventions, which may be initially confusing, are generally celebrated by the cognoscenti for their reality.

William Archer, for example, was committed to the reality of the proscenium-arch stage—as opposed to the platform stage—and even defended the "fourth wall" convention on the grounds that "Nature having omitted to provide us with eyes in the backs of our heads, we can never see more than three sides of a room at once";[13] and we are disposed to accept "stream of consciousness" not because of some agreement which we have concluded with James Joyce or Virginia Woolf, but because it is a convention which meshes silently and unobtrusively with our own sense of reality—so silently and unobtrusively, in fact, that early critics, as Leon Edel points out, had some difficulty in recognizing that it was a convention and not reality itself.[14] It may be that some conventions are no more than matters of theatrical convenience, or necessity, but in the remainder of this essay I would like to consider the possibility that the Elizabethan dramatic conventions governing character meshed as silently and unobtrusively with Elizabethan reality as "stream of consciousness" does with our own.[15]

13. Archer, p. 20.
14. Leon Edel, *The Psychological Novel: 1900–1950* (New York, 1955), p. 30.
15. Dessen, "Elizabethan Audiences and the Open Stage," discusses a number of conventions which can, perhaps, be fully explained in terms of theatrical convenience—ways of indicating stage darkness, for example: " . . . an Elizabethan dramatic company would have used dialogue, torches, nightgowns, groping in the dark, and failures in 'seeing', all presented in full light, to establish the illusion of darkness for a viewer who

I

Cultural anthropology has confirmed the suspicion, which has troubled Western society since Montaigne, that human nature is not a universal which exists independent of a social context. Even the claim of Freudian psychology to be ahistorical has been discredited. [16] Radically different social arrangements simply cannot be derived, as Freud and his successors would have it, from a single, unchanging psychic reality. Culture and psyche are dependent variables, and neither can be reduced to a function of the other. [17] As is now well known, Freud's Viennese patients, upon whose revelations he based his conception of human nature, were suffering from complex tensions which were the product of a particular society in which it was extraordinarily difficult to acknowledge one's sexuality, and for this reason sexuality appeared to be at the basis of all neuroses. [18] "It is always bedroom secrets," whispered Breuer to Freud. [19] But the fact that these revelations were sexual was a historical, not a universal, phenomenon. Even the Oedipus complex—the son's overmastering desire, which must be repressed at all costs, to displace the father in the affections of the mother—appears upon close examination to be a historical phenomenon,

---

presumably would infer night from such signals and stage behavior. For us, the lighting technician supplies stage night . . . " (p. 4). No extratheatrical explanation is called for to account for the differences in Elizabethan and modern lighting conventions. But is this equally true of, say, the unlocalized stage? Dessen observes that "To the original audience, 'place' was an adjunct of the narrative, not an end in itself" (p. 10), which suggests that more is at stake than "assumptions about theatrical presentation" (p. 4).

16. See especially chap. 3 of J. H. van den Berg's *The Changing Nature of Man: Introduction to Historical Psychology* (New York, 1961), pp. 115–188.

17. In addition to van den Berg see Fred Weinstein and Gerald M. Platt, *Psychoanalytic Sociology: An Essay on the Interpretation of Historical Data and the Phenomena of Collective Behavior* (Baltimore, Md., 1973), and Zevedei Barbu, *Problems of Historical Psychology* (London, 1960), which deal with the necessity of steering a course between Marx and Freud, the necessity, that is, of describing the world without either reducing society to the projection of the forces of the psyche or the forces of the psyche to mere responses to social conditions.

18. Van den Berg, pp. 132 ff.

19. Quoted in van den Berg, p. 131.

depending upon a kind of family structure which, at least in the modern world, did not exist before the nineteenth century. [20]

It is for reasons such as these that we are justified in speaking of Elizabethan reality as different from our own in ways which traditional accounts of the period have largely ignored. Modern scholarship, for example, has been much more successful in tracing the romantic quest for new sources of meaning as it has led, in the present century, to the innermost recesses of subjectivity, than it has been in describing the world as it was felt or experienced prior to the romantic movement. The emotional landscape of romanticism is familiar because the forces which shaped romanticism still determine the shape and quality of emotional and intellectual life today. The emotional landscape of the English Renaissance, however, remains elusive and indistinct despite the sophisticated and indispensable accounts of the "Elizabethan world picture" which have been given to us by E.M.W. Tillyard, C. S. Lewis, Theodore Spencer, and others. (We still have almost no idea, for example, what kind of experience inspired Sidney's *Astrophil and Stella*, or the bulk of Shakespeare's sonnets.) We need to go beyond the history-of-ideas approach and examine the medium in which metaphors such as the great chain of being, which many of our students (and colleagues) find merely quaint and comfortable, retained their validity. To do so it is necessary to abandon our assumptions about a universal human nature, which presumably underlies cultural superstructures, and recognize, in the words of one literary historian, "that human formulations and institutions, including our own, are contingent

20. In a lengthy reconsideration of the debate over whether the Oedipus complex is universal or not, Anne Parsons concludes that a more meaningful question would be "what is the possible range within which culture can utilize and elaborate the instinctually given human potentialities, and what are the psychologically given limits of this range?" "Is the Oedipus Complex Universal? The Jones-Malinowski Debate Revisited and a South Italian 'Nuclear Complex,'" *The Psychoanalytic Study of Society*, III (1964), 326. The potential is always there, in other words, but without necessarily being fulfilled. The family structure which actuates it in our society, by throwing father and son into competition for the affections of the mother, has been described by Weinstein and Platt in *The Wish To Be Free* (Berkeley, Calif., 1969), pp. 144–148.

phenomena without any independent reality of their own."[21] The difficulty of taking this final step should not be underestimated. For one thing, it is to venture into territory which has not been very thoroughly explored; and for another, it is very hard to accommodate our concrete experience to the intellectual conviction that this experience is not universal.

Thus J.I.M. Stewart (pp. 69 ff.) puts the case for the relativity of human nature as forcefully as possible, and yet proceeds to analyze Shakespeare's characters, one after another, as if they were our contemporaries. And J. Leeds Barroll, more subtly, argues that though the patterns that Shakespeare perceived, rightly or wrongly, as governing human behavior, were shaped by an ideology radically different from ours, underneath it all lie laws of human nature that are as unchanging as the laws governing the physical universe. Such laws, as revealed by post-Freudian theory and experiments, "must necessarily be taken as applicable retroactively . . . "[22] I should like to argue, nevertheless, that the discrepancy between "unrealistic" dramatic conventions—the impenetrability of disguise, the bed trick, the calumniator credited, inadequate or inconsistent motivation—and dramatic action and characterization which strike us as essentially "realistic," reflects an important difference between Elizabethan reality and our own.

This difference lies principally in the experience of self, and of self in relationship to social roles. The term "identity," by which we designate this experience, owes its present currency to Erik Erikson, one of whose important contributions has been a schema or developmental framework which enables us to perceive cultural differences which have hitherto attracted little attention. Kenneth Kenniston emphasizes this in an article based on Erikson's schema which insists upon the importance of recalling, with the help of developmental psychologists, historians, and anthropologists, "how profoundly different has been the human experience of growing up in other societies and other times—and how different, as a result, was the inner experience and mind-set of adults in other places and

21. D. W. Robertson, "Some Observations of Method in Literary Study," in *New Directions in Literary History*, ed. Ralph Cohen (Baltimore, Md., 1974), p. 67. This is reprinted from *New Literary History* I (October, 1969), 21–33.

22. *Artificial Persons*, p. 11

eras;" [23] and the historical nature of the experience of self has been recognized by both historians and sociologists:

Inasmuch as identity is always part of a comprehensive world, and a humanly *constructed* world at that, there are far-reaching differences in the ways in which identity is conceived and, consequently, experienced. Definitions of identity vary with overall definitions of reality. Each such definition, however, has reality-generating power: Men not only define themselves, but they actualize these definitions in real experience—*they live them*. [24]

Modern response to Elizabethan characters—especially to those who seem most "realistic"—is shaped and complicated by an experience of self which is quite un-Elizabethan. Erikson conveys the sense of this experience—"psychosocial identity"—by two examples which illustrate the distance between our own age and Shakespeare's. The first, an example of the "subjective sense" of identity, is from a letter by William James to his wife:

A man's character, he [James] wrote in a letter, is discernible in the "mental or moral attitude in which, when it came upon him, he felt himself most deeply and intensely active and alive. At such moments there is a voice inside which speaks and says: *'This* is the real me!"

The second, which illustrates the social aspect of identity, is Freud's isolated reference to "an 'inner identity' that he shared with the tradition of Jewry and which still was at the core of his personality, namely, the capacity to live and think in isolation from the 'compact majority.' " [25] This experience of self, even in its "social" manifestation, as deep inner

23. *Journal of Interdisciplinary History*, II (1971), 341–342.

24. Peter Berger, Brigitte Berger, and Hansfried Kellner, *The Homeless Mind: Modernization and Consciousness* (New York, 1973), pp. 91–92. Cf. Karl Weintraub's "Autobiography and Historical Consciousness," *Critical Inquiry*, I (1975), 821–848. Although Weintraub rather nervously disassociates himself from all psychological schools and from "psychohistory" (p. 834), his study supports the position quoted in the text.

25. "Psychosocial Identity," in *The International Encyclopedia of the Social Sciences* (New York, 1968), VII, 61. Erikson's examples are from James's *Letters* (Boston, 1920), I, 199, and Freud's "Address to the Society of B'nai B'rith" (1926), printed in *The Standard Edition of the Complete Psychological Works of Sigmund Freud* (London, 1959), XX, 272–274.

reality or inner core was foreign not only to the Elizabethan (and medieval and Platonic) conception of personality as a hierarchical organization of reason, passions, and appetites, but to Elizabethan reality itself, which was essentially social and public. It was, as many scholars have observed, the age of the enacted idea, an age of pageantry and spectacle. [26] Reality was "out there," so to speak, in a cosmic order which was reflected in the social and ecclesiastical hierarchies, in public architecture (including theaters), in the institution of the family, and even in the organization of personality.

Modern reality, by contrast, is essentially personal and private. The difference can be traced to any of the forces which have shaped the modern world—industrialization, Protestantism, the centralization of political power, urbanization, scientific technology—but whichever of these is singled out as *primus inter pares*, the result is the same: the individual has been forced to turn inward, to create significant order and purpose out of his own inner resources, and hence to experience ultimate reality as something within himself. The old metaphors which expressed ultimate reality in terms of transcendence are so inadequate to this experience that a bishop of the Church of England has suggested, following Paul Tillich, that they be replaced by metaphors of depth, and in fact they have. [27] God is no longer up in his Heaven, but inside us, down in the depths, in the "ground of our being," to use Tillich's famous formulation, which brings to mind the subterranean regions explored by "depth" psychologists. The external, cosmic frame of reference which, however much it had been undermined by the intellectual revolution of the seventeenth century, was still available to Pope when he wrote the *Essay on Man*, was not available to Wordsworth when he set out to write *The Prelude*; [28] and in the scientific view of the universe which replaced it the external world was reduced, as

26. See, for example, C. S. Lewis, *Spenser's Images of Life* (Cambridge, Eng., 1967), pp. 1–17; George R. Kernodle, *From Art to Theatre: Form and Convention in the Renaissance* (Chicago, 1944), chap. 4 and *passim;* Theodore Spencer, *Shakespeare and the Nature of Man*, 2d ed. (New York, 1949), pp. 63–64. Kernodle focuses more sharply on the difference between modern and Renaissance individualism in "The Open Stage: Elizabethan or Existentialist?" *ShS*, XII (1959), 1–7.

27. John A. T. Robinson, Bishop of Woolwich, *Honest to God* (London, 1963), reprinted as *Honest to God and the Debate* (London, 1964), pp. 22, 46.

28. See Basil Willey's famous essay, "On Wordsworth and the Locke Tradition," in *The Seventeenth Century Background* (New York, 1953), pp. 293–306.

Professor Whitehead has put it in a much quoted passage, to "a dull affair, soundless, scentless, colourless; merely the hurrying of material, endlessly, meaninglessly." [29] The world that people thought they were living in—a world richly sensuous and purposeful—had to be internalized in order to survive the new philosophy.

It is easy enough, of course, to observe that earlier ages were less self-conscious than our own, but built into this observation is the assumption that the inner core was really there after all, lying inaccessible— happily unnoticed by all but a few—just below the bright surface of consciousness. But this is precisely the assumption that has been challenged, and there is ample evidence to suggest that the inner core or *ens realissimum* which we experience so concretely is not an unchanging psychic reality but a response to particular historical circumstances which did not exist in the sixteenth century. I shall draw attention to three of these circumstances: childhood, privacy, and autonomy.

Childhood. Childhood memories are the bread and butter of psychoanalysis. The general theory of human existence that came out of Freud and Breuer's work on neurosis is that "Everything has a meaning: the man who forgets something means something by it; the man who makes a mistake in writing is expressing his most secret thoughts; if he arrives at an appointment too early, there is some reason for it; if he arrives too late, that, too, has its deeper meaning." [30] And this meaning is always located firmly in the past, firmly *within*, that is, in some inaccessible childhood episode which is being unconsciously recapitulated. That this is not simply a theory about things but a mode of experience is borne out by the findings of psychoanalysts and by the absolutely critical significance of childhood memories in modern literature—a significance which had already become clear before Freud's discoveries, most notably in the writings of Rousseau and in the poetry of Wordsworth. The inner core *is*, in an important sense, the child within us, whose traumas are the "fountain light" of our neuroses. We tend to assume that this mode of experiencing the past is universal, but in fact it has a history. As Philippe

---

29. *Science and the Modern World* (New York, 1967), p. 54 (chap. 3). This is cited by Willey in *The Seventeenth Century Background* (p. 19), and supported by a similar passage from E. A. Burtt's *The Metaphysical Foundations of Modern Physical Science* (London, 1932), pp. 236–237.

30. Van den Berg, p. 120.

Ariès, the French social historian, has demonstrated in *Centuries of Child-hood*, it was not until the sixteenth and seventeenth centuries that child-hood began to be recognized as a separate and unique stage of life, and not until the eighteenth that this recognition became widespread. And this was not due to an inexplicable failure on the part of parents and educators to perceive that children are essentially different from adults, which is what Rousseau and Wordsworth, in their own ways, both perceived.[31] It was because children and adults occupied the same world, shared the same psychological space, in a way which did not survive the crisis of modern-ity. The thesis which is documented in *Centuries of Childhood* is this:

In the Middle Ages, at the beginning of modern times, and for a long time after that in the lower classes, children were mixed with adults as soon as they were considered capable of doing without their mothers or nannies, not long after a tardy weaning (in other words, at about the age of seven). They immediately went straight into the great community of men, sharing in the work and play of their companions, old and young alike.[32]

The measure of the gulf which has opened between the world of the child and the world of the adult is adolescence, which is perhaps the most critical and difficult phase in the modern life cycle, but which has no counterpart in earlier times.[33] Rousseau mentions a "rather short" period of maturation which corresponds, in a way, to our period of adolescence, but no one before him mentioned it. There is little data on the subject, as van den Berg has pointed out, because it wasn't a subject:

In 1808 the word *Flegeljahre* (awkward age) appeared for the first time in a German dictionary; it had been used as a title for a book by Jean Paul four years earlier. It seems probable that the phase of life described by this expression had appeared only a short time before. Muchow, who mentions these facts, dis-

31. See *ibid.*, p. 71; Philippe Ariès, *Centuries of Childhood: A Social History of Family Life*, trans. Robert Baldick (New York, 1962), p. 411; and Barbara Garlitz, "The Immortality Ode: Its Cultural Progeny," *SEL*, VI (1966), 639–649, especially p. 647.

32. Ariès, p. 411.

33. See Ariès, pp. 25, 30, 239, 329; and van den Berg, pp. 25–38. Cf. Geoffrey Hartman's contention that "it is the Romantics who first explored the dangerous passage-ways of maturation." "Romanticism and Anti-Self Consciousness," in *Romanticism and Consciousness*, ed. Harold Bloom (New York, 1970), p. 47.

covered, after examining biographies and autobiographies, that in none of these life stories was there even one word on the psychic symptoms of puberty or the years of adolescence. We now know why: there was nothing to see then on the border between youth and maturity to ever induce comment. "Childhood is one of the great discoveries of the eighteenth century." And Victor Hugo's remark, "Columbus only discovered America; it was I who discovered the child," was not entirely untrue—he was only mistaken in the ownership of the copyright. The child had not existed before him, and he only came into being later on; he was created by us. Our adulthood has acquired such a peculiar shape that the child has to be childlike if he is ever to reach us; he has to get through a complicated period of psychic maturation before we adults can get the impression that he is really with us—that he really can take part in our complicated, inwardly contradictory but nonetheless, and even partly because of it, so delightful maturity.[34]

The child within us derives his extraordinary strength—his ability to shape our identity—from this gulf which separates the adult world from his own; for as Freud himself always insisted, it is the *inaccessible* past that exercises its sway over us. Elizabethan childhood, however, was not inaccessible, for there was nothing to correspond to the modern division of experience into separate kingdoms with such radically differing laws and customs that only those with special training (psychoanalysts) or special insights (artists) can freely commute between them.

Privacy. As I have already noted, in contrast to modern identity Elizabethan identity was essentially social and public. This was because Elizabethan experience was essentially social and public. Given the lack of privacy it could hardly have been otherwise. "The historians taught us long ago," says Ariès, "that the king was never left alone. But in fact, until the end of the seventeenth century, nobody was ever left alone. The density of social life made isolation virtually impossible."[35] It would be a mistake to conclude that privacy was an ideal that was simply unattainable for most people, as it is for slum dwellers today, for there is good reason to believe that, in an age when even the bedding of a bride was a public affair, privacy was not a meaningful concept. The division between dwelling place and working place, which effectively separates our own world into public and private spheres, had not yet come into being;[36] and it is not

34. Van den Berg, p. 72.
35. Ariès, p. 398.
36. Peter Laslett, *The World We Have Lost*, 2d ed. (New York, 1971), p. 14.

until the eighteenth century, in fact, that a desire for privacy is manifested in houses designed with specialized, independent rooms to create space for private life; and in a code of manners which emphasized "the need to respect the privacy of others" as opposed to the "art of living in public and together"; and in a craving for domesticity which implies a sharp distinction between public and private life.[37]

Autonomy. In the Elizabethan concept of the universe as a system of interlocking hierarchies there was simply no room for the isolated individual, and in practice the autonomy which we prize so highly was virtually nonexistent. Almost no one lived independently:[38] "the idea of service," as Ariès says, "had not yet been degraded. One nearly always 'belonged' to somebody. . . . Society still appeared as a network of 'dependencies'."[39] Burckhardt's famous distinction between medieval man, who "was conscious of himself only as a member of a race, people, party, family, or corporation—only through some general category,"[40] and the individual who emerged in the Renaissance needs to be glossed here, for the individual he describes bears little or no resemblance to the images of man which haunt us today. His individuality was rooted not in Existential *angst* or Marxist alienation but in a social context which survived the Renaissance, though not the economic and political transformations of the eighteenth and nineteenth centuries. It continued to be shaped by a conflict, not between the State and the individual, but between the State and the small groups—corporate family, guild, village community, university, monastery, parish—which once competed with the State for the political, economic, legal, and moral allegiance of the individual.[41] These groups were more or less systematically destroyed in post-Revolutionary France, but even without the vigilance of the French reformers

37. Ariès, pp. 398–401. Cf. John Demos's remarks on privacy in Puritan New England in *A Little Commonwealth: Family Life in Plymouth Colony* (New York, 1970), pp. 46–47.

38. Laslett, p. 11 and *passim*. Cf. Demos, p. 78.

39. Ariès, p. 396; cf. Laslett, p. 5.

40. *The Civilization of the Renaissance in Italy,* trans. S.G.C. Middlemore (London, 1951), Part II, chap. 1.

41. See Robert Nisbet, *The Quest for Community* (London, 1969) (also issued in 1962 with the title *Community and Power*), pp. 109–120 and *passim*, especially chap. 10. See also David Riesman, *The Lonely Crowd* (New Haven, Conn., 1950), p. 14.

they have either disappeared or have ceased to mediate effectively between the State and the individual. Society is no longer a collection of groups but a vast "aggregate of morally autonomous, psychologically free, individuals." [42]

II

The modern experience of self as private and autonomous, shaped by an inaccessible past, differs radically from the experience of self in the Elizabethan social context and distorts our responses to dramatic characters conceived in this social context. This distortion is greatest when we construe the relationship between Elizabethan identity and Elizabethan social roles in terms of our own experience. In the modern world social roles come between us and reality. They are defenses which enable us to hide our true selves from others, who are, of course, protecting themselves by similar defensive strategies. One's true identity is discovered, for good or for ill, by stripping the self of these defensive roles in order to reveal an inner core, the "real" person behind the mask—a process which the self-help books of our time endeavor to facilitate. Elizabethan identity, by contrast, was experienced not in opposition to but by participation in social roles; or rather, social roles were the means not of avoiding but of participating in reality, as one joins in a dance, to use one of the most important Elizabethan metaphors for cosmic and social reality. [43] Ivan Ilych's role as judge, in Tolstoy's modern story, undermines his true humanity; Angelo's unredeemed humanity, in *Measure for Measure*, undermines his transpersonal role as judge.

This difference has been analyzed, in a sociological study, in terms of honor *vs.* dignity. Honor, a social concept which enjoys relatively little

42. Nisbet, p. 228 (and 112). This account of things is not an exercise in nostalgia for a communal past. As Peter Laslett observes in *The World We Have Lost*, the patriarchal arrangements of pre-industrial Europe exploited and oppressed people quite as remorselessly as capitalism. The fact remains, however, that there were important "differences in the manner of oppressing and exploiting" (p. 4), and like more sentimental scholars Laslett insists on the primary importance of the small groups which shaped the lives of people on all social levels. Cf. Nisbet, p. viii, and Riesman, pp. 13–14.

On the French Revolution see Nisbet, pp. 158–175.

43. See E.M.W. Tillyard, *The Elizabethan World Picture* (London, 1943), chap. 8.

prestige in the modern world though it was a matter of first importance to the Elizabethans, implies that one's identity is essentially linked to roles, whereas dignity, which has replaced it, implies the opposite, implies, that is, that identity is independent of roles:

> In a world of honor, the individual discovers his true identity in his roles, and to turn away from the roles is to turn away from himself—in "false consciousness," one is tempted to add. In a world of dignity, the individual can only discover his true identity by emancipating himself from his socially imposed roles—the latter are only masks, entangling him in illusion, "alienation" and "bad faith."[44]

This difference has been illustrated concretely in Stephan Greenblatt's biography of Sir Walter Ralegh, which bears the subtitle "The Renaissance Man and His Roles." Greenblatt shows that at the center of various important Renaissance works—Vives's *Fable about Man*, Pico's *Oration, The Book of the Courtier*, and even *The Prince*—is the idea of shaping an identity or role that is more real than the "natural man" which it supersedes: "The prince, like the courtier, is all surface; he is the actor completely fused with his role." There is no "real" self behind the mask, "there is nothing but a chaos of infinite desire."[45] Ralegh's own life can best be understood in these terms. His letters are "miniature stages on which to perform";[46] his roles—courtier, soldier, adventurer, the queen's lover, discoverer of a golden world—were his realities. Even his death—an occasion on which we expect all false roles to drop away, as they do in the case of Ivan Ilych—was a theatrical event, and this was not atypical: "The truly memorable death scenes of the age, on the scaffold, at home, or even on the battlefield—Sir Thomas More, Mary Queen of Scots, Sir Philip Sidney, John Donne, Ralegh, Charles I—were precisely that: *scenes*, presided over by actor-playwrights who had brilliantly conceived and thoroughly mastered their roles."[47]

Shakespeare's treatment of kingship provides the clearest dramatic

---

44. Berger et al., pp. 90–91.

45. Stephan Greenblatt, *Sir Walter Ralegh: The Renaissance Man and His Roles* (New Haven, Conn., 1973), p. 40.

46. *Ibid.*, p. 23.

47. *Ibid.*, p. 15.

illustration of this mode of experience. The divinely sanctioned role of king was, of course, the most challenging and demanding which this theatrical age had to offer, and England's queen, as many scholars have noted, played this role to the hilt, a fact which was perfectly clear in her own time. [48] But the full significance of Elizabeth's "role-playing" has been obscured by the modern assumption that roles are disguises of an underlying reality. Greenblatt gives a very different account of kingship, however, as does Anne Righter in *Shakespeare and the Idea of the Play*. Both insist on the reality of the role:

In the ceremony of coronation, an individual assumes what is essentially a kind of dramatic role, a specific part which he must interpret, but which he may not, in its fundamental respects, change. It is a part, however, with which he is completely identified thereafter, from which he cannot be separated except by violence. [49]

The doctrine of the king's two bodies was not a deliberate mystification but a logical formulation of this experience.

The most recent lengthy discussion of this subject, Thomas Van Laan's valuable *Role-playing in Shakespeare*, [50] provides a great deal of evidence to support this position, though like Greenblatt and Righter he does not confront directly one of the most powerful and satisfying alternative approaches to Shakespearean roles: namely, the view that in Shakespeare what we witness is reality itself breaking through and destroying the social roles and conventions that were meant to contain it. Theodore Spencer, for example, speaks of Shakespeare's "repeated emphasis on the human reality underneath the outer cover of ceremony." [51] The evidence on which he bases this observation admits more than one interpretation, however. Henry V's brooding, on the night before the battle of Agincourt, is undeniably congenial to our way of thinking: "the king is but a man," says Henry, distinguished from the wretched slave and the beggar only by Ceremony, which can procure for him neither health nor a good night's

48. *Ibid.*, pp. 53–54.
49. (London, 1962), pp. 113–114.
50. (Toronto, 1978).
51. Spencer, p. 84.

sleep. [52] The reality which the play as a whole affirms, however, is not that of the "real" man emerging from behind a false mask, but of the young Henry fulfilling his kingly role beyond all hope and expectation. The reality of this role is first questioned and then affirmed.

Richard II is more complex. According to Spencer, Shakespeare introduces the traditional views of kingship as illusions to be dispelled, "showing how a king who has accepted those views discovers, with a kind of sentimental desperation, that human suffering is the reality underneath." [53] The human suffering is real enough, but Spencer is too quick to deny the reality of the role. Richard does not discover, in the deposition scene, that his kingly role was illusory; he discovers that outside the role he has no identity, a fact which is emphasized dramatically by the breaking of the glass. And when, in his final scene, his identity is reaffirmed, it is reaffirmed not in terms of Richard the man, asserting his "real" self against false roles, but in terms of his kingly role:

> That hand shall burn in never-quenching fire
> That staggers thus my person. Exton, thy fierce hand
> Hath with the King's blood stain'd the King's own land.
>
> (V.v.109–111)

Bolingbroke and Macbeth make similar discoveries about the roles which they assume—roles which prove, like Richard's, not to be illusory, but too real to be sustained. Bolingbroke cannot wear his crown with ease, and Macbeth's role, as the well-known studies of clothing imagery in the play have demonstrated, is like an ill-fitting garment. [54] *King Lear* offers an even closer parallel. The moment at which Lear divests himself of his royal apparel in order to join Edgar is not the moment of truth but, as Madeleine Doran has astutely observed, "the moment of his complete loss of reason." [55] "The thing itself, unaccommodated man," is not the reality

52. IV.i.101. All references are to *The Riverside Shakespeare*, ed. G. Blakemore Evans (Boston, 1974). Spencer discusses this passage on pp. 82–84.

53. Spencer, p. 76.

54. Cleanth Brooks, "The Naked Babe and the Cloak of Manliness," in *The Well Wrought Urn* (New York, 1947). Brooks draws upon Caroline Spurgeon, *Shakespeare's Imagery and What It Tells Us* (Cambridge, Eng., 1935).

55. Doran, p. 63.

which is disclosed in the play, for Lear's tattered identity, like Richard's, is eventually reasserted: "The trick of that voice I do well remember," says Gloucester on the heath; "Is't not the King?" "Ay," answers Lear, "every inch a king!" (IV.vi. 107).

This experience of self also underlies another kind of dramatic role-playing—disguise (under which heading I would also include bed tricks). I have said little about disguise since the orthodox interpretation of the "impenetrability of disguise" in terms of its dramatic utility has not been seriously challenged by psychologically oriented critics, probably because it is, even in the most serious contexts, simply too unbelievable to invite the kind of psychological interpretations which can always be found for inadequate or inconsistent motivation. [56] "The stage conventions," says Miss Bradbrook, "did not attempt to make it convincing, but it had simply to be accepted." [57] But we are entitled to ask, why did it *have* to be accepted? Why were Elizabethan audiences able to swallow certain uses of disguise which have choked modern critics?—the failure of Gloucester to recognize his own son, the failure of Florizel to recognize his own father, the failure of Bussy to recognize the disguised Montsurry in Chapman's *Bussy d'Ambois*, the failure of Bertram and Angelo to recognize Helena and Mariana.

Miss Bradbrook's account of disguise in *Elizabethan Tragedy*, cited above, is not very illuminating; in another essay, however—one of the remarkably few devoted to the Elizabethan use of disguise—she gives a penetrating answer to this question. For one thing, she argues, "there was an 'open' or unresolved view of individuality behind Elizabethan character-drawing, which corresponded to the open use of words in Elizabethan poetry." Character, like language, was fluid, and a role might vary "from a specific or strictly individual one to something nearer the function of the Greek chorus." [58] And for another, the important physical basis of disguise rested on an unmodern assumption: "Apparel was not thought of as concealing but as revealing the personality of the wearer. . . . Hence there

---

56. Little has been done to supersede Victor Freeburg's *Disguise Plots in Elizabethan Drama* (New York, 1915).

57. Bradbrook, p. 66.

58. Bradbrook, "Shakespeare and the Use of Disguise in Elizabethan Drama," *Essays in Criticism*, II (1952), 163.

could be no such thing as a mere physical transformation. As the body revealed the soul, so appearance should reveal the truth of identity. A character could be really changed by the assumption of a disguise." [59] Disguise, then, was all of a piece with a larger whole. For Miss Bradbrook this larger whole consists of literary practice and beliefs about "apparel," which is accurate, but too circumscribed; for disguise was in fact a special kind of role-playing—one that cannot be adequately explained in terms of dramatic utility since it is equally prevalent in Elizabethan nondramatic literature—which was particularly suited to the Elizabethan experience of self, not as inner core, shaped by an inaccessible past, but as dramatic role to be played in the *theatrum mundi.* Without claiming that "impenetrability of disguise" was "realistic" in the modern sense, we can say that it chimed with Elizabethan reality, which does not emerge when the imprisoned self is released from inhibiting social roles, but when the proper or true role has been assumed—when Malevole discloses himself to Pietro in *The Malcontent,* or when Lucio pulls off a friar's hood and discovers a duke.

III

The discrepancy between realistic character portrayal and apparently unrealistic literary conventions cannot be reconciled by modern depth psychology. The persistent search for an inner core by which to render inadequate and inconsistent motivation intelligible is doomed from the outset, not because Elizabethan dramatists found it convenient to dispense with psychology, as "conventional" critics maintain, but because what we experience as inner core is not an unchanging psychic reality but a response to particular historical circumstances which did not exist in the sixteenth century. Elizabethan identity, as I have described it above, was much less internalized than our own. It could, therefore, house forces which cannot cohabit comfortably in the restricted inner space of the more highly integrated modern personality, which is why Elizabethan heroes often strike us as "larger than life." When such cohabitation occurs today, as it frequently does, the result is quite different, for one of the parties is generally forced

59. *Ibid.,* pp. 165–166.

to decamp to the cellar where, to borrow a metaphor from Freud, he may continue to disturb the household "by his outcries and by hammering on the door with his fists." [60] The metaphor engages us, but it is inappropriate to the Elizabethan experience of self.

Othello's willingness to credit Iago, on the one hand, and his generous and unsuspicious nature, on the other hand, present a problem only when we conceive of Othello's actions and characteristics as rays of light which, however they are refracted by various circumstances, nonetheless emanate from a single inner source. The same is true of Hamlet's inconsistencies, which have excited such an alarming amount of psychological interest, or the Duchess of Malfi's, to take the most celebrated non-Shakespearean example of a character real enough to invite, but problematic enough to resist, modern psychological interpretations. The conviction, in all these instances, that there is a "real" Othello, or a "real" Hamlet, or a "real" Duchess of Malfi, who cannot be perceived directly but whose existence can be inferred from the confused and contradictory evidence of the text, is understandable because it is based on our own experience of reality. The failure of modern depth psychology to give credible accounts of these "real" characters supports the thesis, put forward here, that Elizabethan experience was radically different from our own and that no such characters ever existed.

The alternative does not lie in "conventional" explanations, for the compelling reality of these characters cannot be derived, as Professor Stoll would have it, from artificial and outworn devices which are bound by only the slenderest of threads to actual human experience. It lies in recognizing that the essence of Elizabethan identity lay not in an inner core but, as Stephan Greenblatt has put it in the biography of Sir Walter Ralegh

60. Sigmund Freud, "The Origin and Development of Psychoanalysis," trans. Harry W. Chase, *American Journal of Psychology*, XXI (1910), 195. This series of lectures is reprinted in vol. XI of *The Standard Edition of the Complete Psychological Works of Sigmund Freud* (London, 1957).

A Rumanian psychologist, Zevedei Barbu, has also argued that a distinguishing feature of the Elizabethan personality—in real life as well as drama—was its ability to combine character traits which seem incompatible, to us, and that a "psycho-cultural" interpretation is called for. His own interpretation, which differs radically from my own, is based on the assumption, which I think unjustified, that the "morally rigid medieval world" had collapsed. *Problems of Historical Psychology* (London, 1960), pp. 172–179 and *passim*.

cited above, in man's "power to commit himself to a role and thereby transform his own nature. . . ."[61] In Othello's commitment to his heroic role Greenblatt finds the same dialectic that shaped Ralegh's life and writings—"the full commitment of the self to a role which is yet recognizable as a role."[62] Van Laan's more detailed account of *Othello* leads to the same conclusion. At the end of the play Othello recreates the heroic identity that Iago has managed to destroy by re-establishing his heroic role.[63] The psychological interpretations of Othello which I have mentioned are inadequate because they deny the reality of the role itself. Othello's nobility is reduced to self-delusion and his encounters with good and evil to "projections." The trouble with this, as J.I.M. Stewart has observed, is that the play offers no psychological entity answering to this description of Othello, whose heroic role is not a disguise but "a reality set magnificently before us in both Venice and Cyprus."[64] It is this role that Iago succeeds in undermining:

> Farewell the plumed troops and the big wars
> That make ambition virtue! . . .
> Farewell! Othello's occupation's gone.
>
> (III.iii.349–357)

What emerges is not the "real" Othello, but chaos. Chaos is not, however, the ultimate reality, for in the calm at the end Othello's "heroic identity, the greatness of heart by which he had forged a place for himself in Venice," is recovered by "the single grand, histrionic act left to him: he kills himself as he had once killed the hated Turk."[65]

Hamlet should be understood in similar terms, and has been, in fact, in a number of studies for which this essay endeavors to provide a theoretical basis.[66] Hamlet's world is not shaped by his Oedipus complex. His iden-

61. Greenblatt, p. 51.
62. *Ibid.*, p. 50.
63. Van Laan, p. 180 ff.
64. Stewart, p. 105.
65. Greenblatt, p. 50.
66. It would be difficult to write about *Hamlet* without touching upon some aspect of this question. Two recent studies which focus specifically on the question of Hamlet's role are Paul Gottschalk's "*Hamlet* and the Scanning of Revenge," *SQ*, XXIV (1973), 155–170,

tity is problematic because his role is problematic, and it ceases to be problematic when, having confronted the most powerful symbols of man's mortality, he commits himself to a role which is eventually touched by the suggestion of God's providence, but which is immediately expressed in social terms:

> This is I,
> Hamlet the Dane!
>
> (V.i.217–218)

Likewise the Duchess of Malfi. Stripped of all possessions and prerogatives, all symbols of rank, confronted with her own death, she puts the all-important question to her executioner: "Who am I?" "Worm-seed," he answers, "green mummy," "Crudded milk, fantastical puff paste." She is not shaken, however, and her most concrete experience of self is asserted, as it is time and again in Elizabethan literature, not in terms of the "real" person behind the mask, but in terms of a transpersonal role:

> "I am Duchess of Malfi still!"
>
> (IV.ii.139)

The dramatic conventions which I have described are based on an experience of self quite different from our own. They strike us as problematic or unrealistic because they do not accord with our experience of self as inner core. These conventions, however, are all of a piece with Elizabethan identity; they merge imperceptibly with a reality which, though less subterranean, was perhaps more capacious than our own. Elizabethan drama is a window through which we can see this reality if we are not too preoccupied trying to catch our own reflection in the glass.

---

and Stanford M. Lyman and Marvin B. Scott's *The Drama of Social Reality* (New York, 1975), chap. 2. See also Peter Alexander, *Hamlet, Father and Son* (Oxford, 1955), chap. 5, and Helen Gardner, "The Historical Approach," in *The Business of Criticism* (Oxford, 1959).

Once again, I have found my own position confirmed by Van Laan, who interprets *Hamlet* in terms of the difficulties Hamlet experiences in (1) resisting the roles which others would thrust upon him and (2) discovering his own authentic role (pp. 173–176).

Elizabethan Lighting Effects and the Conventions of Indoor and Outdoor Theatrical Illumination

R. B. GRAVES

I T IS AN ARTICLE OF FAITH among theater historians that dramatists generally write with an eye toward production and that expected performance conditions will affect the composition of the play. In comparing the verse of Thomas Kyd and James Shirley, say, we have to take into account not only two different temperaments at two different points in the development of English poetry, but also two different kinds of theatrical environments—the large, outdoor "public" playhouses and the small, indoor "private" playhouses. Thus when Shirley in "A *Prologue at the* Globe *to his Comedy call'd* The doubtfull Heire, *which should have been presented at the* Black-Friers" complains that actors at the open-air Globe were forced "to break our lungs" in contrast to the easily heard speech at Blackfriars, [1] we do not need to explain the difference between the ranting of Kyd and the slick proficiency of Shirley solely by recourse to perceived shifts in social and literary fashion from Elizabethan to Caroline times. The acoustics of their respective theaters must have influenced, in part at least, the kind of language appropriate to each. In a similar way, it has long been assumed that the general lighting of the playhouses (daylight at the public

1. James Shirley, *Poems &c.* (London, 1646), pp. 154–155. Shirley had originally written the play for the indoor Werburgh Street theater, Dublin, which apparently was similar to the Blackfriars.

theaters, a mixture of daylight and candlelight at the private theaters) must have affected the manner in which dramatists used stage property lights and special lighting effects. Stage directions call for familiar candles, tapers, lanterns, and torches, as well as such curiosities as suns, moons, blazing stars, strokes of lightning, and burning cities. Most of these have been described by W. J. Lawrence, Lee Mitchell, and others, together with assessments of their functions as stage images. [2] It is not my purpose to go over the same ground again. Rather, I wish to focus on the relationship between property light and the over-all illumination in the theater. Further, I should like to examine whether playwrights used property lights differently in the public and in the private theaters. For unlike many stage properties, hand-held lights and special lighting devices were more or less dependent upon the general theatrical environment for their effect, and a dramatist's expertise in using such property lights cannot be measured without reference to the over-all light on stage.

In taking up such questions, several difficulties arise immediately which make it doubtful that any definitive conclusions can be reached. The most troubling problem is that we often do not know which plays may be considered public and which private. The assurance on a title page, for instance, that a play was acted indoors or outdoors ought never be ignored, of course, but on the other hand it is not proof that a printed stage direction calling for a property light does not derive from a promptbook prepared for a different venue of production. For example, W. A. Armstrong has taken the stage direction in Henry Chettle's *The Tragedy of Hoffman*, "*Enter as many as may be spar'd, with lights,*" to imply that the

2. Lawrence's essays, "Light and Darkness in the Elizabethan Theatre," in *The Elizabethan Playhouse*, II (Stratford, 1913), 1–22, and "Characteristics of Platform Stage Spectacle," in *Pre-Restoration Stage Studies* (Cambridge, Mass., 1927), pp. 251–276, recount the major effects with a wealth of examples. Mitchell centers on "Shakespeare's Lighting Effects," *Speech Monographs*, XV (1948), 72–84, and classifies them by chronographic, symbolic, ceremonial, and metaphoric functions. Brownell Salomon, "Visual and Aural Signs in the Performed English Renaissance Play," *RenD*, V (1972), 163–164, follows in Mitchell's footsteps with a semiological view of property lights in non-Shakespearean drama. Alan C. Dessen, "Night and Darkness on the Elizabethan Stage: Yesterday's Conventions and Today's Distortions," *RenP, 1978* (1979), pp. 23–30, demonstrates the complexity of transferring Renaissance lighting conventions to the modern stage.

general illumination was not strong at the indoor Cockpit in Drury Lane, where the title page of the first edition says it was acted.[3] Armstrong ascribes this direction to a desire to supplement the playhouse candles with extra lights brought on stage. But who wrote this stage direction, and to what time and place does it refer? The tentative phrase, *"as may be,"* suggests it was written by the author and not by whoever prepared the authorial text for production. We know from Henslowe's diary that the Admiral's Men paid Chettle for the play as early as 1602.[4] In this case, the stage direction may reflect production at the outdoor Fortune theater, that is, if Chettle was thinking of a certain theater in the first place.[5] On the other hand, the play bears evidence of revision, no doubt for its revival indoors at the Cockpit around 1630. Did the reviser write this stage direction, taking poor indoor light into account? One is inclined to doubt it, because he presumably would have known the resources available and would not have been so vague. And in any event, the stage direction does not necessarily point to a desire for more illumination. These lights are brought on for a formal scene of mourning at night, only forty-two lines long, near the end of the play. The *"as many as may be spar'd"* more likely arises from a wish for ceremony and spectacle, while the lights themselves represent an attempt to indicate pretended darkness on a daylit stage.

A better example for Armstrong comes from Marston's *What You Will*, almost certainly written for the Paul's Boys around 1601 and published in 1607, after the company had disbanded and relinquished its rights to the play. In the last act, a stage direction reads, *"Enter as many Pages with Torches as you can"* (sig. H1ᵛ). But again the theatrical situation reveals that Marston was primarily employing torches as signals for the coming of night and for the preparations preceding the play-within-a-play about to be performed. As the torches are carried on stage, a courtier explains, "Seace the Duke approacheth tis almost night . . . lightes lightes now ginnes our play." These lights are brought on only some 150 lines before

---

3. Armstrong, *The Elizabethan Private Theatres* (London, 1958), p. 12; *Hoffman* (1631; rpt. London, 1951), sig. H.

4. *Henslowe's Diary*, ed. R. A. Foakes and R. T. Rickert (Cambridge, 1961), p. 207.

5. R. A. Foakes, "Tragedy at the Children's Theatres after 1600," in *The Elizabethan Theatre II* (Hamden, Conn., 1970), p. 52, sees an early children's-theater influence in the play.

the end of the play. One would think that if the playhouse illumination was consistently so dark as to warrant extra stage lights, they would have been introduced a good bit sooner. Perhaps these torches compensated for waning daylight at the end of the play: we know that around 1601, the Paul's Boys' plays lasted until 6 P.M., that is to say, well more than an hour past winter sunset.[6] Certainly such lights might have appeared more spectacular as evening approached, but one searches in vain for a pattern of children's plays which brought on lights at the end. Had phrases like "so many as may be" regularly referred only to torchbearers, one might view their purpose differently. But such phrases occur frequently without any mention of lights. A stage direction for a wedding procession in Robert Armin's *The Two Maids of More-clack*, "*Enter . . . some other women for shewe*," gives a simpler reason for the employment of the largest cast possible.[7]

Thus we encounter another problem in dealing with property lights—namely, we cannot always tell what their functions were supposed to be. Did the author of these stage directions want more light on stage, or did he merely want more characters and paraphernalia? Was it the torchlight that produced the sense of ceremony or only the large number of attendants holding lighting utensils? I doubt that Marston, Chettle, or Chettle's reviser saw any need to differentiate these functions; but for our purposes, we may distinguish among three roles which property lights played in relation to the general illumination—roles which I shall call illusionistic, realistic, and emblematic.

By illusionistic, I refer to stage light which attempted to duplicate lighting in the real world: dark for night, bright for day, artificial light for indoors, natural light for out of doors. The criterion here is whether the playwright attempted to approximate images the audience would recognize. By realistic, I refer not to verisimilitude of the illumination but to

6. See William Percy's note quoted in J. P. Collier, *Annals of the Stage* (1831; rpt. New York, 1970), III, 377.

7. *The Two Maids of More-clack* (London, 1609), sig. A1ᵛ. Later, in a welcoming ceremony, lords and ladies parade over the stage "*so many as may be*" (sig. H2ᵛ). Such indefinite and "permissive" stage directions (usually without lights) are common and associated with authorial, rather than playhouse, intentions; see W. W. Greg, *The Shakespeare First Folio* (Oxford, 1955), pp. 135–138.

the use of property-lighting instruments as realistic detail. In this second role, torches or tapers did not accomplish their theatrical purpose by means of light, but by their appropriateness to the scene and the authenticity with which the actors used them. They were, or could be, telling physical objects which one would or would not find in certain places at given times. Whether or not Lady Macbeth's taper accurately reproduced the lighting of a castle at Dunsinane, for example, it nevertheless "realistically" signaled such information as the time of the sleepwalking scene (night), the place (indoors, since tapers were rarely used outside), and even the circumstances that her walk was unplanned and that she goes not as the self-assured queen we have seen heretofore (here the lady of the castle is not accompanied by the usual retinue of attendants lighting her way). By emblematic, I refer to uses of property lights not strictly verisimilar but figurative. Extensions of this category would include various iconographic associations—Lady Macbeth's taper construed as a token of her loneliness, for example—but mainly I have in mind the use of such lights as suns, moons, stars, and comets as signs of night and day, order and disorder, and the like.

Sometimes property lights serve theatrical purposes in two or three modes at once. In scenes of pomp, for instance, the introduction of many richly garnished lights could throw enough artificial light on the scene to create the illusion of the artificial light at a noble entertainment in a hall. The lighting instruments themselves could contribute to the realistic decoration of the scene. And one might argue that, in some cases, the glittering torches emblematized the artifice and unnaturalness of the courts, for example, during such ironic masques as those in *Women Beware Women* (V.ii), *The Maid's Tragedy* (I.ii), and even the Mousetrap play in *Hamlet*. In these scenes, illusion, realism, and emblems work together to produce a concert of visual meaning. When torchbearers entered "so many as may be," the playwrights wanted both brilliance and a crowded stage, as well as some of the sophistication associated with torchlight.

But in the more prevalent use of stage lights as a means of evoking darkness, the three modes can easily work against each other. Light emitted by the instruments brought on stage to add realistic detail obviously prevented the illusionistic depiction of night. The remarkable aspect of the use of property lights in both the public and private theaters is that indications of darkness were effected by the introduction of more, rather than less, light onto the stage. Light paradoxically represented darkness, and as such must be accounted not illusionistic. But in another sense, the deployment of property lights about the stage was very realistic, because real people do light candles and torches when it gets dark. In other words, the action on stage was real enough, even though the illumination on stage was not. When torches and tapers were carried on stage to indicate that a scene was supposed to take place at night, the theatrical statement was that an *instrument* of light had been called into use. It was the instrument, or rather the imaginary need for the instrument, and not the light it produced that represented the darkness. One cannot imagine that the torchlight in the Queen Mab scene of *Romeo and Juliet* or in the opening scenes of *Othello*, for example, would have been particularly striking on the daylit Globe stage. Both plays were originally intended for production out of doors, where such torchlight (not to mention the feeble light of Lady Macbeth's taper or the light Othello carries into Desdemona's chamber) would have been nearly invisible. On windy days especially, the actors might even have had difficulty in keeping open-flamed candles and tapers lit. Perhaps the actors never even bothered to light some of these utensils, since the light of the flames added little to, indeed worked against, the evocation of darkness.

Yet in the private theaters one would think that the illumination provided by stage lights was sometimes illusionistic, because it was the same light which illuminated all halls at night. W. J. Lawrence, for one, was convinced that in regard to stage lighting "the Elizabethans paid a good deal more attention to the science of stage illusion than we give them credit for." At one time Lawrence believed that the "rear stage" was in such an obscure position that the audience's "inconvenience . . . almost invariably demanded the bringing-in of lights at the commencement of all inner [stage] scenes." Later Lawrence changed his mind and admitted that lights were brought on just as frequently for "outer" scenes. But he continued to argue that the inner stage and tiring-house wall made the artificial illumination emanating from these brought-on lights look more real.[8] He insisted that the rear stage, as used in "study" or "bedroom"

8. *The Elizabethan Playhouse*, I (Stratford, 1912), 6–7; II, 2–3.

scenes, looked more like a real study or bedroom at night because of the artificial property-light that had been introduced. Similarly, Harley Granville-Barker thought that Imogen's taper in the bedroom scene of *Cymbeline* was doubly effective because it not only helped to symbolize her chastity but also joined with the candelight already present to produce the illusion of the intimate artificial light in her bedroom. [9]

But the general illumination of any theater had to shine alike on both indoor and outdoor scenes. If we follow Lawrence's and Granville-Barker's theory to its logical conclusion, then we should have a situation where indoor scenes were played illusionistically at Blackfriars and realistically (that is, conventionally) at the Globe, while outdoor scenes were played illusionistically at the Globe and realistically at Blackfriars. There is a marginal increase of indoor scenes in the more sophisticated children's-theater drama, but not an inkling of a reversal in the conventions of lighting as the actors performed more and more indoors. Distinctions in location were effected by what I am calling realism, not by illusion. When a scene was supposed to take place indoors, lights designed for indoor use were brought on. By far the most common light introduced into a scene Lawrence calls an "inner" scene is the taper. Tapers were single, thin ropes dipped in tallow, which had the advantage of not dripping hot tallow nor of requiring snuffing as true candles did. Hence they were used as night-lights in bedrooms, where they could burn safely with little attention paid to them. Like Imogen and Lady Macbeth, Evadne (*The Maid's Tragedy* V.i), Clarinda (*Love's Progress* III.i), and Merione (*The Queen of Corinth* III.ii) have tapers by their beds. When the scenes shift to outdoors, torches and lanterns replace tapers. Whether the audience was to think of the scene as indoors or outdoors was determined by the *type* of lighting utensil, not by its light. The illumination did not make the scene look authentic; rather the utensils engaged the actors in realistic business. It would have been impossible to tell where a scene was supposed to occur by the light a taper threw out at the daylit Globe, and difficult enough at the windowlit Blackfriars. In using the shape of the utensils rather than the quality or quantity of the light they produced to help set the scene, the actors were consequently free to use the same staging in whatever general

9. *Prefaces to Shakespeare* (Princeton, N.J., 1946), I, 472.

light they found themselves. On bright or dark days, indoors or outdoors, in the afternoon or at night at Court, hand-held lights could signal the time and location of scenes because their effect was independent of the over-all illumination.

In the private theaters, then, where one might have expected that lights carried on stage were used to amplify the existing light, the same practice of indicating darkness by the occasional introduction of property lights took hold. By far the majority of stage lights suggested imaginary darkness, just as they did outdoors. Blackfriars plays such as *The Elder Brother* (IV.iii), *Love's Pilgrimage* (I.ii), *The Fair Maid of the Inn* (I.i), *The Maid of the Mill* (I.iii; IV.iii), and *The Knight of Malta* (IV.ii), as well as a host of probable Blackfriars plays like *Alphonsus of Germany* ("*Enter* Alphonsus *the Emperour in his night-gown, and his shirt, and a torch-in his hand* "), [10] use stage lights to indicate darkness, not to increase the sense of brightness in the play or the theater. So too, Cockpit plays like Shirley's *The Maid's Revenge* (III.vi), *The Witty Fair One* (IV.iv), *The Wedding* (IV.iv.), and *The Lady of Pleasure* (III.i) employ stage lights exactly as they are used in the outdoor theaters—to represent darkness. The interesting corollary to this conclusion, moreover, is that despite the attempt to suggest darkness, there had to be enough light on stage for the audience to see what kind of lighting utensil was brought on, as well as to see other important signals of time, place, and character which had nothing to do with light.

Corroboration that the evocation of darkness was not illusionistic comes from Shakespeare's satire of the mechanicals' naïve representational expectations in III.i of *A Midsummer Night's Dream*. In preparing for their entertainment before Theseus and Hippolyta, Quince points to the major obstacle for the realistic presentation of their play: "that is, to bring the moonlight into a chamber; for you know, Pyramus and Thisby meet by moonlight." Snug, Bottom, and the others are literalists; they insist on consulting an almanac to learn whether the moon will be shining on the

10. *Alphonsus, Emperor of Germany* (1654; rpt. New York, 1913), sig. B. In assigning plays to Blackfriars and the Cockpit in Drury Lane, I follow T. J. King in citing plays whose stage directions probably reflect actual stage practice there; see King's "Staging of Plays at the Phoenix in Drury Lane," *TN*, XIX (1965), 149–150, and his review article of Irwin Smith's *Shakespeare's Blackfriars Playhouse*, in *RenD*, IX (1966), 297–299. See Dessen, p. 24, for the relationship between lights and other signs of night.

night of their play. When they happily discover that the moon will indeed be out, Bottom finds the solution to the problem simple: "Why then may you leave a casement of the great chamber window (where we play) open; and the moon may shine in at the casement." Bottom contends that moonlight may best be represented by the real thing, but Quince, who has had more experience in these matters, believes that the emblematic approach is better. He suggests, "or else one must come in with a bush of thorns and a lantern, and say he comes to disfigure, or to present, the person of Moonshine." [11]

The joke rests in part on the fact that no one champions the method of representing night which Elizabethan playwrights used most often—the realistic mode. No one suggests that a few token properties associated with night be brought on stage. Bottom proposes an illusionistic technique which is patently absurd. But although we may find Quince's emblematic solution just as ludicrous, there is reason to believe that the Elizabethans found it less so; or at any rate, considered a man holding a lantern only a little less sophisticated than other emblems for night—representations of moons and stars, for example. [12]

Such emblems were most popular before the turn of the century, but they continued throughout the period. Among the Admiral's Men's properties, inventoried in 1598, for example, was "the clothe of the Sone & Mone." [13] What this was is not clear: it may have resembled the costumes which dressed Phoebus and Persephone in Thomas Heywood's *Ages* plays for Queen Anne's Men, [14] or it may have been some sort of painted emblem of day and night along the lines of the Admiral's Men's own "sittie of Rome." In the last act of *1 Troublesome Reign of John*, Philip the

---

11. III.i.48–61. Except as noted, citations from Shakespeare are from *The Riverside Shakespeare*, ed. G. Blakemore Evans (Boston, 1974).

12. An eyewitness description of English actors in Germany ca. 1626 recounts the scene with slightly different emphasis. Real moonshine is never considered, but a red and yellow paper moon and one made of rotten wood which glows in the dark are. The mechanicals conclude that the most "natural" method is a lantern "hung on a butchers' skewer, which one of us will carry and move along with it a little every quarter hour"; see Ernest Brennecke, *Shakespeare in Germany* (Chicago, 1964), p. 65.

13. *Henslowe's Diary*, ed. Foakes and Rickert, pp. 319–320.

14. Allan Holaday, "Heywood's *Troia Britannica* and the *Ages*," *JEGP*, XLV (1946), 437.

Bastard casts his eyes up "to heauen" and sees "Fiue Moones reflecting, as you see them now." Were these moons only imaginary? To make it explicit, we get the stage direction, "There the fiue Moones appeare." [15] The play is early, Chambers assigning it to the Armada period of 1588, [16] but we cannot say definitely that it was performed indoors or outdoors. The title page says it was "*acted by the Queenes Maiesties Players, in the honourable Citie of* London." If both Chambers and the title page are correct, then the play may well have been produced at the Bel Savage Inn; but the history of the Queen's Men is sufficiently unclear that we must include the possibility of the Bull and Bell Inns, as well as the Theatre and Curtain, these last two not strictly in the City, however. If the play was performed at the Bel Savage, then it may or may not have been performed indoors. At any rate, when Shakespeare wrote the same scene for outdoor production in his *King John*, these physical moons were eliminated and their appearance only narrated. Perhaps Shakespeare avoided such effects for the same reasons he ridiculed the admittedly more simpleminded lantern-emblem in *A Midsummer Night's Dream*.

We are left wondering, though, what these five moons looked like. There were lighting utensils called "Moons" in the Renaissance; according to the nineteenth-century antiquarian Thomas Wright, they were globe-shaped lanterns. [17] George Kernodle is positive the effect in *1 Troublesome Reign* was produced by "a machine which made one moon whirl about the others, to symbolize England and her scorn of popish lands," on the none-too-relevant authority of similar machines in Continental *tableaux vivants*. [18] Of these possibilities, neither the Admiral's Men's cloth nor Kernodle's machine can be thought of as lighting effects as such, because they emblematize night in pictorial rather than in luminary terms. Wright's Moon lantern and Quince's lantern are true lighting utensils, but unless they were employed in darkened halls, they too would achieve their effect less by light than by symbolism. Like realistic property lights, to the extent that successful emblems of night did not depend on light alone,

---

15. *1 Troublesome Reign of John* (1591; rpt. London, 1911), sig. G2^v.

16. E. K. Chambers, *The Elizabethan Stage* (Oxford, 1923), IV, 23.

17. *A History of Domestic Manners and Sentiments in England During the Middle Ages* (London, 1862), pp. 454–455.

18. *From Art to Theatre* (Chicago, 1944), p. 142.

they afforded a flexible means of indicating night, which worked as well outdoors as indoors.

Other important emblems associated with night were the star and blazing star or comet. These may be traced back to the nativity stars in medieval religious drama. The York, N-Town, and Chester shepherds' plays specifically require stars for their productions, which presumably took place out of doors, although it has recently been argued that these Corpus Christi plays may have been performed indoors. [19] Stars were also featured in the Chester Cathedral in liturgical plays. Late churchwarden's accounts there list several payments pertaining to stars. In 1553, the Cathedral "payd for the starr ij^s," and in 1558 "for a pully to the starr & setting it vp 4^d." [20] The London Cordwainers had three "greatt stars" for their Bethlehem pageant "with iij^{re} glasses and a cord for the same steris." [21] Similar stars on cords were used at Yarmouth in Norfolk from 1462 to 1512. Churchwarden's accounts there include "making a new star," "leading the star," and "a new balk line to the star and ryving [pulling?] the same star." [22] With the Reformation, nativity stars went out of fashion, but I doubt that stars on lines and pulleys did. Again these stars appear to have been painted effects rather than burning lights. We read nothing of tallow or wax for them, and one would think it dangerous to be pulling burning lights along lines suspended above the parishioners. The Cordwainers' stars with "glasses" might be some sort of lamp; but *glass* more likely refers to a mirror. Probably pieces of glass glittered on the stars, reflecting back the existing light in the church.

Most of the stage directions calling for stars in the professional theater occur early in the period and would, therefore, refer most often to open-air productions. But again, indications are that stars were used both outdoors and indoors. In a dumb show in *The Battle of Alcazar*, there is thunder and lightning as Iris descends from the heavens. Then comes the stage direction, *"Heere the blazing Starre."* [23] The Presenter of the dumb show elaborates:

19. Alan H. Nelson, *The Medieval English Stage* (Chicago, 1974), pp. 65 ff., 114, and 159.

20. F. M. Salter, *Mediaeval Drama in Chester* (Toronto, 1955), p. 17.

21. Hardin Craig, "The London Cordwainers' Pageant," *PMLA*, XXV (1917), 606.

22. E. K. Chambers, *The Mediaeval Stage* (Oxford, 1903), II, 399.

23. [George Peele,] *The Battle of Alcazar* (1594; rpt. London; 1907), sig. F.

"Now firie starres and streaming comets blaze," after which another stage direction calls for *"Fire workes,"* and the Presenter continues, "Fire, fire about the axiltree of heauen, / Whoorles round." The play was published in 1594 as acted by the Admiral's Men, but it had passed to them from the Lord Strange's Men's repertory at the Rose a few years earlier. But in a brilliant piece of minute detective work, W. W. Greg has shown that the 1594 text is based on an extensively cut version prepared for provincial touring. Comparing the published play to the surviving backstage "plot," which probably reflects stage practice at the Rose, Greg finds that much of the original spectacle has been eliminated and the cast reduced. However, he finds evidence that the stage direction calling for the blazing star was part of the original full-length version performed at the Rose. [24] Because the effect was not cut by the reviser, it presumably could be handled both outdoors at the Rose and indoors in the provinces, where most plays were performed in halls and inns.

Blazing stars are almost always associated with fireworks and may well have been fireworks themselves. The trouble with fireworks is that they are dangerous and cause unpleasant odors. These problems may have raised little concern for the dramatists at the outdoor theaters, but indoors it must have been otherwise. The Prologue to Shirley's *The Doubtful Heir*, cited earlier, proudly proclaims that since the play had been intended for Blackfriars there would be no squibs in it. The principal reason for this avoidance of fireworks is best explained by metaphors in two children's private-theater plays which compare improvident gallants to "squibs running vpon lines" which "Stink." [25] If blazing stars were fireworks, we might tentatively conclude that they could only be used outdoors. Such is the opinion of Inga-Stina Ewbank, who in the continuing controversy over the authorship of *The Revenger's Tragedy*, offers the blazing star in V.iii as evidence that the play was written for outdoor production at the Globe and, hence, cannot have been written by Middleton for the children at Blackfriars. [26] Her argument for attribution to Tourneur turns on

24. *Two Elizabethan Stage Abridgements* (London, 1922), p. 117.

25. Thomas Dekker and John Webster, *Northward Ho!* (1607; rpt. London, 1914), sigs. F3^v-F4; and John Marston, *Parasitaster, or The Fawn* (London, 1606), sig. B, reproduced by University Microfilms, Ann Arbor, Mich. In subsequent notes UM = University Microfilms.

26. "A Note on 'The Revenger's Tragedy,'" *N&Q*, cc (1955), 98–99.

Chambers's remark that in comparison to the Red Bull and its elaborate fireworks, "The Globe, with its traditional 'blazing star', is left far behind." [27] She takes Chambers to mean that blazing stars were more characteristic of the Globe than anywhere else. But Mrs. Ewbank has misunderstood Chambers. By "traditional," he meant only that blazing stars were old devices, and that in the competition for new spectacle, the Globe had not kept pace with other playhouses. He does not mean that blazing stars were unique to the Globe; indeed, I have been unable to find one play, other than *The Revenger's Tragedy*, which contains a blazing star and is associated with Globe production. [28]

Although most blazing stars are associated with the Rose and Red Bull, we cannot entirely discount their use indoors. Both the manuscript and quarto versions of Thomas Goffe's *The Courageous Turk* call for blazing stars, and the manuscript states that the play was acted 21 September 1618 by students of Christ Church, Oxford, presumably indoors. [29] The stage history of *If You Know Not Me, You Know Nobody* is confused, but there is a strong possibility that the second part or sections of it was performed at the Cockpit in Drury Lane around 1630. [30] Quartos published before and after this revival have stage directions calling for blazing stars. *Thorney-Abbey* may not have been performed before the Interregnum, but its two stage directions calling for blazing stars appear to have been intended for indoor production, because a stage direction at the end of the play calls for the playhouse candles to be extinguished. [31] One would think that fireworks as elaborate as blazing stars were avoided at the private theaters, and it is true that fewer and fewer new plays contained blazing stars as the period neared its end. But the old plays continued to be revived

27. *The Elizabethan Stage*, III, 110.

28. See D. L. Frost, *The School of Shakespeare* (Cambridge, Eng., 1968), pp. 259–260. At the Globe on 23 May 1633, Sir Humphrey Mildmay saw John Fletcher's *Rollo*, which describes a descending "bright starre," which may or may not have been shown. The play was frequently revived indoors—at Court, at the Cockpit in Drury Lane, and after the Restoration; see *Rollo* (1639; rpt. London, 1948), p. 67, and G. E. Bentley, *The Jacobean and Caroline Stage* (Oxford, 1941–1968), I, 109, and II, 695.

29. *The Courageous Turk* (London, 1632; rpd. UM), sig. H; and Bentley, IV, 506.

30. Chambers, *The Elizabethan Stage*, III, 342–343; Madeleine Doran, ed., *If You Know Not Me* (1606; rpt. London, 1934), Part I, xii–xv, and Part II, xi and sig. E2ᵛ.

31. *Gratiae Theatrales* (London. 1662), sig. B7 and *6ᵛ.

indoors and out. On the whole, we may say that blazing stars may have been presented less elaborately and less often indoors, but their decline in popularity may as easily be traced to the Jacobean distaste for the naïve emblems of the Elizabethans as to the Jacobean fondness for indoor theaters. There is certainly no evidence to suggest that blazing stars were used exclusively at the public theaters; nor, in fact, any proof that they were lighting effects in a strict sense of the term.

It is interesting to note that most of the blazing stars occur late in the plays. I give their positions in redacted acts and scenes: *Battle of Alcazar*, V; *Captain Thomas Stukeley*, V; *The Birth of Merlin*, IV.v; *The Revenger's Tragedy*, V.iii; *2 If You Know Not Me*, III; *Rollo*, V; *The Courageous Turk*, V. Could it be that blazing stars were meant to look more real in the gathering darkness at the end of the play? Or were they simply delayed so that the general rise in dramatic interest was paralleled by an increase in spectacle? An appearance of three suns early (II.i) in the bad quarto of *3 Henry VI* might argue likewise that suns would look more natural in the bright afternoon light. In the authentic Shakespearean version, Edward exclaims, "Dazzle mine eyes, or do I see three suns?" while Richard gives a long description of "Three glorious suns" coming together to become "one light, one sun" (II.i.25–31). But in the pirated (or, perhaps, adapted) version, Richard's narration is trimmed considerably, and a stage direction added: "Three sunnes appeare in the aire." [32] What these suns looked like is even more difficult to imagine than what moons looked like. It seems unlikely that the English had any lights at their disposal which could have produced convincing suns out of doors. [33] Perhaps something on the order of the Admiral's Men's "clothe of the Sone" was employed, a technique effective in nearly any theatrical environment.

Outdoors, and perhaps indoors, fireworks were often employed for their

32. *True Tragedy of Richard Duke of York* (1595; rpt. London, 1891), sig. B3ᵛ.

33. Continental effects were evidently more sophisticated. For a 1539 open-air play in the great courtyard of the Medici palace at Florence, e.g., Aristotile de San Gallo created a sun, approximately two-feet high, made of a crystal ball filled with water behind which two torches shone. The sun was controlled by a windlass so that it rose to the zenith by the middle of the comedy and sank in the west by the end. Giorgio Vasari claimed it "looked like a veritable sun"; *The Lives of the Painters, Sculptors and Architects*, trans. A. B. Hinds (New York, 1927), III, 296–297.

own sake without regard to associations with night and day. *Doctor Faustus*, performed at the Rose and Fortune, is familiar evidence. Yet one wonders how effective fireworks were in the daytime, whether indoors or outdoors. Fireworks are clearly better at night. The noise they produced could be appreciated at any time, but not their brilliance. The conjecture that certain plays may have been performed late in the day because they included fireworks suggests itself, but without evidence. We do know that at the Beargarden in Southwark (ca. 1584), fireworks were apparently delayed until the conclusion of the day's games.[34] And a look at *Doctor Faustus* shows six uses of fire and fireworks with a distinct progression of more and more elaborate spectacle toward the end. For this play, perhaps, Marlowe may have been aware that it might be wise to delay the big lighting effects until the sun was beginning to sink. Thus through the first four acts of the 1616 B text (Greg's divisions), fireworks are used only to frighten people—the Pope, his Cardinals, and the soldiers. This fright can be accomplished by the noise of the fireworks alone, for we should remember that Elizabethan fireworks did not produce the long-lasting, brilliantly colored displays we enjoy. In *The Broken Heart*, Ford makes the point that fireworks commonly produced their effects by noise, not by light: "So squibs and crackers flye into the ayre, / Then onely breaking with a noyse, they vanish / In stench and smoke."[35]

But in the final scene of *Doctor Faustus* when "*Hell is discouered*"[36] (apparently the "Hell mought" included in the Admiral's Men's 1598 inventory), we know that something more than noise was resorted to. Probably the audience saw none of what the Bad Angel describes (an ever-burning chair, damned souls being tossed on forks, bodies broiling in lead) except in their mind's eye, but the Admiral's Men did not leave everything to the imagination, either. We are fortunate to have two contemporary accounts of the play's catastrophe. In *Astrologaster*, John Melton tells of a performance at the Fortune before 1620: "a man may behold shagge-hayr'd Deuills runne roaring ouer the Stage with Squibs in their mouthes, while Drummers make Thunder in the Tyring-house, and

---

34. Chambers, *The Elizabethan Stage*, II, 455.
35. *The Broken Heart* (London, 1633; rpd. UM), sig. D2.
36. Christopher Marlowe, *The Tragical History of Doctor Faustus* (London, 1616; rpd. UM), sig. H2.

the twelue-penny Hirelings make artificiall Lightning in their Heauens." [37] And in his satire on warfare, *Worke for Armorours*, Thomas Dekker mentions that in one battle "wilde fire flew from one [army] to another, like squibs when Doctor *Faustus* goes to the diuell." [38] Much or all of the effect of the burning in hell might have been represented by the smoke of the fireworks, although neither Melton nor Dekker mentions smoke. Artificial lightning from the heavens could have been produced by a number of methods. Both flames and strokes of lightning were sometimes produced by powdered rosin thrown or blown past a burning torch. This technique was popular early in the period, but like the blazing star fell into some disrepute later, even though it was cited as the correct method for making lightning in the 1611 English edition of Sebastiano Serlio's *Architettura*. [39] In 1599, the King's Men's *A Warning for Fair Women* disdainfully recalled the crowd-pleasing spectacles of Marlowe and Kyd:

> Then of a filthie whining ghost,
> Lapt in some fowle sheete, or a leather pelch,
> Comes skreaming like a pigge halfe stickt,
> And cries *Vindicta*, reuenge, reuenge:
> With that a little Rosen flasheth forth,
> Like smoke out of a Tabacco pipe, or a boyes squib. [40]

Again it is clear that rosin flashes produced more smoke than light. As late as 1636, however, Richard Lovelace in the Epilogue to *The Scholars*, a Whitefriars play, was still complaining about some of the audience's love for this spectacle. Lovelace avers he should have written two plays instead of one—the first for the yokels in the galleries and another for the more discriminating gentlemen in the pit:

> The first for th' Gallery, in which the Throne
> To their amazement should descend alone,
> The rosin-lightning flash, and Monster spire
> Squibs, and words hotter than his fire. [41]

37. *Astrologaster* (London, 1620; rpd. UM), sig. E4.
38. *Worke for Armorours* (London, 1609; rpd. UM), sig. F4.
39. See Barnard Hewitt, ed., *The Renaissance Stage* (Coral Gables, Fla., 1958), p. 35.
40. *A Warning for Fair Women* (1599; rpt. London, 1912), sig. A2^v.
41. *The Poems of Richard Lovelace*, ed. C. H. Wilkinson (Oxford, 1930), p. 67. The play itself has not survived.

Lovelace is not quite clear on the matter; evidently rosin flashes could also be used indoors at Whitefriars, although he certainly disapproves of them. Similar disapproval was voiced regarding lightning produced by squibs running on lines. In some quarters, at least, both these effects were considered less refined and less safe than various Continental techniques for representing lightning, which nevertheless did not become popular in England. [42]

Most fires were apparently produced simply by smoke. Literary stage directions of descents into hell mention fiery exhalations and the like, but it would have been dangerous to have real flames emanate from beneath wooden stages. In Robert Wilson's comedy *The Cobler's Prophecy*, the Priest tells us, "The Cabbin of Contempt doth burne with fire," but we know from the stage direction that the effect was actually more modest. In a playhouse stage direction, the tireman was ordered, *"from one part let a smoke arise."* [43] One of the rare playhouse distinctions between smoke and fire is made by stage directions in John Fletcher's *Bonduca*. In III.i we witness a Druid sacrifice during which ceremonies are performed at an altar A stage direction calls for *"A smoak from the Altar,"* and Bonduca duly notes that "The fire takes." But his sister is upset that *"no flame arises."* More prayers are offered, a stage direction reads, *"A flame arises,"* and Bonduca happily announces that "It flames out." [44] Bibliographical analysis of the text shows that these stage directions originated in the playhouse and not with Fletcher, who might only have imagined that the difference between smoke and flames could be demonstrated on stage. From the cast list appended to the play, Chambers can date it to either the 1608–10 or 1613–14 season when the King's Men were performing at both Blackfriars and the Globe. [45] Probably a similar (or the same) trick

42. L. B. Campbell, *Scenes and Machines on the English Stage During the Renaissance* (Cambridge, Mass., 1923), 64–65, 157, describes the classical method of painting lightning on *periaktoi* (which could be spun) or on planks (which could be dropped from the heavens) and a seventeenth-century Italian method of cutting a board lengthwise in a zigzag pattern, and then placing candles behind while the rift between the two sections of the board was opened and closed.

43. *The Cobler's Prophecy* (1594; rpt. London, 1914), sigs. G1ᵛ-G2.

44. Francis Beaumont and John Fletcher, *Comedies and Tragedies* (London, 1647), sig. Hhhh1.

45. R. C. Bald, *Bibliographical Studies in the Beaumont & Fletcher Folio* (London, 1938), p. 78; Chambers, *The Elizabethan Stage*, III, 228.

altar was used at about the same time for the King's Men's Blackfriars play, *The Two Noble Kinsmen*, in which Emilia puts a hind upon an altar and sets fire to it, whereupon the hind disappears and in its place a rose tree ascends (V.i). Or again, a play performed "nine days together at the Globe," Middleton's *A Game at Chess*, requires an altar from which "flames aspire," tapers "set themselves afire," and statues move in a dance.[46] Clearly the use of such altars both indoors and outdoors suggests that playwrights could rely on the audience's readily understanding the same lighting conventions in a variety of lighting environments.

Although fewer and fewer fire and lightning effects were called for in Jacobean and Caroline texts, the decrease cannot be explained solely by the more frequent use of indoor theaters. Early indoor plays—especially those written in the 1560s and 1570s—contain numerous fire effects, an indication that the popularity of such conflagration scenes and effects was determined by taste and fashion as much as by the physical circumstances of production. In 1572, for instance, a wax chandler made an expensive "device in counterfeiting Thunder & Lightning" for a play by the Children of the Chapel at Court.[47] Since a chandler and not a painter was responsible, we must assume that some kind of burning light was used indoors to represent lightning. But other indoor entertainments employed very conventionalized methods of representing fires. In 1566, Queen Elizabeth saw a play at Oxford at night in which a character ascended from hell with "flaming head, feet, arms, which flame was not with fortuitous, but with innate, deep-seated burning."[48] Similar clothing "sprinkled with bloud and flames" is found in the dumb show before Act IV of *Gorboduc*, performed at the Inner Temple, 1561.[49] Perhaps the clothing was flame-colored or was decorated with strips of cloth which resembled flames when the actor moved. Such appears to be the method used in costuming Inigo

---

46. Thomas Middleton, *A Game at Chess*, ed. R. C. Bald (Cambridge, 1929), p. 108.

47. Albert Feuillerat, ed., *Documents Relating to the Office of the Revels in the Time of Queen Elizabeth* (Louvain, 1908), p. 142.

48. W. Y. Durand, *"Palamon and Arcyte," PMLA*, XX (1905), 514.

49. Thomas Sackville and Thomas Norton, *Gorboduc* (1570–1571; rpt. London, 1908), sig. E3.

Jones's fiery spirits for Jacobean masques.[50] In the late morality play, *All for Money*, both Damnation and Judas have garments "painted with flames of fire,"[51] a technique which clearly afforded the troupe a flexible means of staging which would be appropriate in nearly any venue in which they happened to find themselves performing.

In sum, the evidence we have indicates no substantially different use of property lights indoors or outdoors. The contrasts of darkness and light on the English Renaissance stage were first and foremost functions of the imagery in the spoken words and, hence, worked their effects most prominently in the imaginations of the spectators. Many of the lights brought on stage may never have been lit or may have produced their effect by conventional symbolism. It is all too easy to overestimate the allusive power of light used on stage by means of selective citations. Most of the plays use no lights at all, and of those that do, the majority use lights simply as realistic detail. Property lights were important technical considerations, but less because of the light they produced than because of the scenes they helped to set. Lights carried by the actors had the ability to participate in the concert of action, language, and theatrical environment by creating moods and, at times, helping to show what, when, and even who was supposed to be on stage. And finally, the use of such property lights and special effects suggests that the stage conditions at the public and private theaters could not have been in such opposition as to oblige dramatists or actors to rewrite plays to fit different lighting systems.

50. See, for example, the costume design in Stephen Orgel and Roy Strong, eds., *Inigo Jones: The Theatre of the Stuart Court* (London, 1973), I, color plate 81, for Thomas Campion's *Lords' Masque*, 1613.

51. T. Lupton, *All for Money* (1578; rpt. London, 1910), sigs. Bij and Eij.

Face-Painting in
Renaissance Tragedy

ANNETTE DREW-BEAR

I·N BARNABE BARNES'S *The Devil's Charter*, Lucretia Borgia, after painting her face on stage, exclaims, "Who painted my faire face with these foule spots, / You see them in my soule deformed blots."[1] Spectacularly and sensationally, this scene acts out the moral consequences of hypocrisy and evil. The poisoned tincture that stings and burns Lucretia's face symbolizes her corruption. Through this distinctive staged action, the dramatist heightens a moral issue central to his play. Although much work has been done to show how dramatists used visual imagery to intensify a play's themes, this particular image of face-painting has not been recognized as a distinctive recurring feature in Renaissance drama.

Recent critics have called attention to "presentational imagery," "emblematic stage imagery," "iconic stage imagery," and "imagery and symbolic action for the viewer's eye."[2] Martha Hester Fleischer, for example, defines stage imagery as persons, properties, and actions which

1. Ed. R. B. McKerrow, in *Materialien zur Kunde des älteren Englischen Dramas,* ed. W. Bang et al., vol. 6 (1904; rpt. Vaduz, 1963), IV.iii.2107–2108.
2. See Maurice Charney, *Shakespeare's Roman Plays: The Function of Imagery in the Drama* (Cambridge, Mass., 1961), pp. 7–8; Martha Hester Fleischer, *The Iconography of the English History Play* (Salzburg, 1974), pp. 1–24, and "Stage Imagery," in *The Reader's Encyclopedia of Shakespeare,* ed. Oscar James Campbell and Edward G. Quinn (New York, 1966), pp. 819–820; John Doebler, *Shakespeare's Speaking Pictures: Studies in Iconic Imagery* (Albuquerque, N.M., 1974), pp. 1–20; Alan C. Dessen, *Elizabethan Drama and the Viewer's Eye* (Chapel Hill, N.C., 1977), pp. 71–109.

function as visible expressions of a play's themes and as visual counterparts of the verbal imagery in the dialogue.[3] No one, however, has called attention to a particular group of images ranging back to the morality plays and forward to the Jacobean tragedies of Webster, Tourneur, and Massinger. A close look at these face-painting images in the plays and at the historical contexts in sermons and moral treatises can help us go beyond our twentieth-century prejudices about cosmetics to a deeper understanding of how face-painting functions to heighten central themes in Renaissance tragedy.

A good point of departure is the symbolic technique of face-spotting, blackening, and whitening which Renaissance dramatists inherited from earlier plays. As T. W. Craik observes, in the Tudor interlude spots "always signify moral corruption."[4] Werner Habicht similarly notes that Wit's "perversion, like that of many morality sinners, is symbolized in physical disfiguration" and face-blackening.[5] *Wisdom* clearly illustrates the morality convention of using facial alteration or disfigurement to symbolize moral corruption. Raymond Williams defines a convention as a "tacit agreement" that is "largely customary" and often "virtually unconscious," expressing "the terms upon which author, performers and audience agree to meet."[6] Following this definition, facial ugliness, deformity—manifested in its extreme form in the ugly long snout or other disfigurement of the devil—was an agreed-upon symbol of moral depravity in the morality play. Thus Lucifer's claim that he will "dysvygure" man, God's image, is represented visually by the deformed Anima, who, the stage directions tell us, "apperythe in the most horrybull wyse, fowlere than a fende."[7] To underscore verbally what is conveyed visually, the

3. "Stage Imagery," in *The Reader's Encyclopedia of Shakespeare*, p. 819.

4. *The Tudor Interlude: Stage, Costume, and Acting* (London, 1958), p. 65.

5. "The *Wit*-Interludes and the Form of Pre-Shakespearean 'Romantic Comedy,'" *RenD*, VIII (1965), 79. In *Mankynde in Shakespeare* (Athens, Ga., 1976), Edmund Creeth remarks that in both *Wit and Science* and in *Wisdom* "black is the emblem of the irrational, the 'abhominable' and devilish, and the blackness of Wyt's smudged face anticipates the sinfulness that Othello finds 'as black as mine own face' and the deed that makes him appear to Emilia 'the blacker Divell'" (p. 17).

6. *Drama from Ibsen to Brecht* (New York, 1969), p. 13.

7. *The Macro Plays*, ed. Mark Eccles, EETS (Oxford, 1969), ll. 353, 902 s.d. I have modernized the thorn.

author of *Wisdom* employs the technique of having a character (Wisdom) point to the deformed Anima and expound on the significance of her ugliness: deformity of face and feature symbolizes deformity of soul:

> Take hede!
> Se howe ye haue dysvyguryde yowr soule!
> Beholde yowrselff; loke veryly in mynde!
>
> (ll. 900–902)

Wisdom's reference to "Howe horryble" the "synnys stynke" (l. 896) suggests that evil smells accompany the spectacle. Wisdom's concluding injunction enforces the connection between disfiguring and devotion to the devil: "Now ye be fayrest, Crystys own specyall; / Dysfygure yow neuer to the lyknes of the fende" (ll. 1113–1114).

Wit and Science shows how the stage action of marking a character's face with black (the fiend's color) is used to symbolize corruption. Stating that her "marke on him shall I clappe,"[8] Idlenes blackens Wit's face. In his mirror scene, Wit himself tells his audience what his black face symbolizes:

> Other this glas is shamefully spotted,
> Or els am I to[o] shamefully blotted.
>
> . . . .
>
> And as for this face, [it] is abhominable,
> As black as the devill.
>
> (ll.806–807, 815–816)

In *The Three Ladies of London*, to "set foorth," as the title page states, "how by the meanes of Lucar, . . . Conscience is so corrupted," that she is "fraught with all abhomination,"[9] Robert Wilson shows Lucre spotting

8. John Redford, *Wit and Science*, in *Medieval Drama*, ed. David Bevington (Boston, 1975), 1. 432.

9. *A Select Collection of Old English Plays Originally Published By Robert Dodsley In The Year 1744*, ed. W. Carew Hazlitt, 4th ed., vols. VI-VII (1874–1876; reissued New York, 1964), p. 246.

Conscience's face with ink from "the box of all abhomination" which is "painted with divers colours, and is pretty to the show" (p. 337). Here the action of face-blackening is also associated with sexual corruption and lust, for Lucre, offering a five-thousand-pound bribe, persuades Conscience to open up her house to all manner of sweet delight, to turn it, in effect, into a bawdy house.

The morality convention of the Vices disguising themselves as virtues also finds visual expression in the devil's masking his black face with a white visor. Lucifer's speech in *Wisdom* points to this convention of the "white devil":

> For, for to tempte man in my lyknes,
> Yt wolde brynge hym to grett feerfullnes,
> I wyll change me into bryghtnes,
> And so hym to-begyle. . . .

(ll. 373–376)

Here the action of disguising the black face with a white visor represents deceitful disguising in order to mislead. [10]

While the face-blackening and whitening in *Wisdom, Wit and Science*, and *The Three Ladies of London* is highly artificial, the face-coloring in Lewis Wager's *The Life and Repentaunce of Marie Magdalene* is not far removed from some actual beauty practices of the time. A variety of paints and washes was available and widely used by the 1550s and even much earlier for both supposed beautifying and symbolic purposes. Red face color appears as a sign of sin in the twelfth-century Benediktbeuern *Passion Play* when Mary asks the Merchant for colors, for rouge to redden her cheeks so that she may entice young men with the thoughts of love:

---

10. On the white devil, cf. 2 Cor. 11:14: "for Satan himself is transformed into an angel of light." See also *Othello*, II.iii.357–358, and Morris Palmer Tilley, *A Dictionary of the Proverbs in England in the Sixteenth and Seventeenth Centuries* (Ann Arbor, Mich., 1950), D231: "The Devil can transform himself into an angel of light"; D310: "The white Devil is worse than the black"; V44: "Vice is often clothed in virtue's habit."

Chramer, gip die varwe mier,
diu min wengel roete,
da mit ich di jungen man
an ir danch der minnenliebe noete. [11]

By the sixteenth-century, products to whiten the face ranged from poison-ous white lead or ceruse to powdered borax, beaten egg whites and egg shells, lemon juice, and ground hogs' bones. A vermilion or red color was supplied by such means as red ocher and mercuric sulphide. Women (as well as men) dyed their hair to the favored blond color by using prepara-tions ranging from honey, wine, and spices to "lead calcined with sulphur, and one part of quicklime" mixed with water. [12]

Wager's play shows how these cosmetic practices were used for symbolic purposes. The Vices act out their seduction of Mary by advising her to paint her face white to cover her "brown" complexion, to "wear a past," and to "curle" and "colour" her hair to keep it "yellow." [13] To disguise any blemish or sign of age, "a Painter on your face would set such an ornature" (l.563), Concupiscence tells Mary, that she "should seeme yong and very faire" (l. 564) and always able to allure "yong men vnto [her] loue" (l. 553). Mary is spotted, perhaps to suggest her syphilitic blotches and the ugliness of sin which face-paint can hide. Infidelity notes that "about here

11. *Medieval Drama*, ed. David Bevington (Boston, 1975), 11. 39–42. Medieval German dramatists expanded the episode in which the merchant sells Mary cosmetics. For example, in *Das Wiener Passionspiel*, in *Das Drama des Mittelalters*, vol. I, ed. Richard Froning (Stuttgart, 1891), the cosmetic discussion is elaborated (p. 315, ll. 287–294), and a devil brings in a mirror to aid Mary's cosmetic application (p. 317, ll. 329–332). A recurring comic elaboration consists of the addition of a doctor/merchant and of his wily servant, Rubinus, who itemizes the ingredients of the cosmetics (mercury, fat, flies' feet) while poking fun at the women who use them. See "Die Krämerscene aus dem dritten Erlauer Spiele," in *Das Drama des Mittelalters*, ed. Froning, vol. I, p. 80, ll. 584 ff.

12. Sir Hugh Platt, *Delightes for Ladies* (London, 1609), p. 102. This popular work went through ten editions between 1602 and 1636. See also Carroll Camden, "Gilding the Lily," in *The Elizabethan Woman* (Houston, 1952); Neville Williams, *Powder and Paint* (London, 1957), pp. 12–32; Richard Corson, *Fashions in Makeup: From Ancient to Modern Times* (London, 1972).

13. Ed. Frederic Ives Carpenter (Chicago, 1902), ll. 546–547, 554–565, 577–579, 602. Infidelitie's song in praise of Mary invites us to "behold" her "face," her golden hair, her "lyps as ruddy as the redde Rose," and her white teeth (ll. 772, 774, 780–781).

nose there be little prety holes" which makes him "thynk that she hath had the pockes" (ll. 571–572). Paint, he assures Mary, would cover these faults. As in the Benediktbeuern play and in other versions of her story, cosmetics symbolize Mary's sexual corruption and her role as seducer of men.

Reacting to the popularity of face-paint in courtly circles, Renaissance moralists continued to use red and white face-coloring symbolically and dramatists exploited these associations in their tragedies. Abstractions such as pride, lust, deceit, and devilish temptation are repeatedly expressed visually by the painted face. When Thomas Nashe describes Pride in *Pierce Penilesse His Svpplication To The Divell*, he presents only "the vglie visage of Pride" whose "picture is set forth in so many painted faces here at home"; and he proceeds to associate the "drugs," "sorceries," "oiles," "oyntments," and "vermillion and white" colors, which "our curious Dames" use to disguise their "withered beauties," with "sin" and "licentiousnesse." [14] Lucifer, too, is pictured in terms of his face—unalterably black despite his appeals to laundresses to whiten it. The connection between the devil's whitening and disguising his face and women's use of deceitful cosmetics is wittily expressed in Nashe's fanciful account of "*A medicine to make the diuel faire*," in which Dame Nature failed to anoint his face with such cosmetics as "*Lac virginis*" and "the oyle of Tartary and Camphire" to whiten it (p. 181). This moral color symbolism occurs again in *Christs Teares over Iervsalem* when Nashe warns women "that howe euer you disguise your bodies, you lay not on your colours so thick that they sincke into your soules. That your skinnes being too white without, your soules be not al black within" (II, 138). At the day of Judgment, God will say: "Sathan, take her to thee, with blacke boyling Pitch rough cast ouer her counterfeite red and white." With glowing hote yrons, sindge and sucke vp that adulterized sinfull beauty, where-with she hath branded herselfe to infelicity" (II, 139,140).

Clearly, red and white paint constitutes a "brand" or sign of sin and lust, a potent visual symbol for the stuff of tragedy. Temptation, too, is expressed by women's painting:

14. *The Works of Thomas Nashe*, ed. Ronald B. McKerrow (Oxford, 1958), I, 180–181.

Euer since *Euah* was tempted, and the Serpent preuailed with her, weomen haue tooke vpon them both the person of the tempted and the tempter. . . . If not to tempt and be thought worthy to be tempted, why dye they & diet they theyr faces with so many drugges as they doe . . . ?

(II, 136–137)

Exhorting women on the subject of face-painting, the authors of the *Book of Homilies* ask: "What other thing dost thou by those means, but provokest others to tempt thee, to deceive thy soul, by the bait of thy pomp and pride?" Castigating "such painted and flourished visages, which common harlots most do use, to train therewith their lovers to naughtiness," the preachers warn women that these acts "do rather deform and misshape thee, than beautify thee." [15]

This repeated linking of cosmetics and deformity indicates that in the Renaissance red and white makeup enhanced the morality convention of using extreme deformity (Anima's horrible features) or black faces and marks to symbolize devilish temptation and corruption. As Thomas Tuke observes, quoting Andreas de Laguna, "The Ceruse or white Lead, wherewith women vse to paint themselues was, without doubt, brought in vse by the diuell." [16] Roger Edgeworth's sermon preached during the reign of Henry VIII details this popular association of cosmetics and devilish perversion, which is also expressed visually in woodcuts showing a devil painting a woman's face:

This adulteration and changing of God's handiwork by painting women's hair to make it seem fair and yellow, or of their cheeks to make them look ruddy, or of their forehead to hide the wrinkles and to make them look smooth, is of the devil's invention and never of God's teaching. [17]

Exploiting such events as the Overbury poisoning, which Frances Howard conceived with the aid of the notorious Mrs. Turner, moralists eagerly pointed to the association between face-painting and the sins of adultery, witchcraft, poisoning, and murder. The common Puritan association of face-coloring with more heinous sins is typified by the second title page of

---

15. *Sermons and Society*, ed. Paul A. Welsby (London, 1970), pp. 62, 61.
16. *A Treatise Against Paint(i)ng and Tincturing of Men and Women* (London, 1616), B3^r.
17. *Sermons and Society*, p. 50.

Thomas Tuke's treatise: *A Discovrse Against Painting and Tincturing of Women. Wherein the abominable sinnes of Murther and Poysoning, Pride and Ambition, Adultery and Witchcraft, are set foorth & discouered* (London, 1616). The makeup which boys wore to play the parts of women lent itself to such dramatic heightening.

To see how these face-painting conventions (agreed-upon associations and actions) were put to use in Renaissance tragedy, consider a relatively unsophisticated play, Barnabe Barnes's *The Devil's Charter* (1607). This play shows in a very straightforward, obvious way how a dramatist could make use of face-painting to highlight or italicize a major theme. Barnes has a penchant for exhibiting what Guicchiardine, the moral presenter, terms "the visible and speaking shewes, / That bring vice into detestation" (III.v. 1697–1698). The prologue alerts the audience to behold the fate of Lucretia, who is poisoned in a spectacular face-painting scene, as an exemplum of God's punishment for sin:

> *Gracious spectators doe not heere expect,*
> *Visions of pleasure, amorous discourse:*
> *Our subiect is of bloud and Tragedie,*
> *Murther, foule Incest, and Hypocrisie.*
> *Behold the Strumpet of proud* Babylon,
> *Her Cup with fornication foaming full*
> *Of Gods high wrath and vengeance for that euill,*
> *Which was imposed upon her by the Diuill.*[18]
>
> (ll. 1–10)

Lucretia is identified with the scarlet whore of Revelations 17 whose branded forehead provides the biblical source for using a marked face to symbolize lust and other sins:

And the woman was arrayed in purple and scarlet color, and decked with gold and precious stones and pearls, having a golden cup in her hand full of abominations and filthiness of her fornication:

And upon her forehead *was* a name written, MYSTERY, BABYLON THE GREAT, THE MOTHER OF HARLOTS AND ABOMINATIONS OF THE EARTH.

(Rev. 17:4–5)

18. Barnes invented the face-painting scene. Lucretia did not die until 1519, whereas the death of Alexander occurred in 1503 (McKerrow, p. 127).

Lucretia's entrance in IV.iii. *"richly attired with a Phyal in her hand"*
(l. 2005) links her clearly with the whore of Revelation and her cup of
fornication. Announcing that her phial contains a precious cosmetic "tincture" sent by her lover, Lucretia calls for "blanching water" to whiten her
face before she applies the color. In an extensive mirror scene, Lucretia, to
correct "a little riueling [wrinkling] / Aboue [her] for-head" (ll. 2021–
2022), orders her maid, Motticilla, to apply "the tincture" and other
cosmetics to her face while *"Shee looketh in her glasse"* (l. 2020) and while
"She looketh in two glasses and beholdeth her body" (l. 2065). As Motticilla
(whose name suggests "spots") washes Lucretia's face with blanching
water, applies the precious tincture ("now will I try these collours"), dabs
on "oyle of *Talck*," smooths her forehead, and plucks her eyebrows,
Lucretia tries to "delay" (dilute by adding water) what she sees as the
"carnation" color imparted by the poisoned tincture (ll. 2062–2066). Rub
as she may, Motticilla cannot correct the singed and repellent face of
Lucretia, symbolic of her whorish sins:

> I feele a foule stincke in my nostrells,
> Some stinke is vehement and hurts my braine,
> My cheekes both burne and sting, giue me my glasse.
> Out out for shame I see the blood it selfe,
> Dispersed and inflamed. . . .
>
> (ll. 2075–2079)
>
> A foule vnsauorie loathsome stinke choakes vp
> My vitall sences. . . .
>
> (ll. 2101–2102)

The audience, which has been led to expect an exemplary vengeance for
Lucretia's incest, fornication, and murder of her husband, watches a spectacle in which the action of applying the red "tincture" from the poisoned
phial, the "cup" of "fornication," visually identifies Lucretia with the
scarlet whore whose multiple sins are branded and burned on her face to
signify her moral and physical death. To enforce the visual image,
Lucretia, like the spotted sinners in *Wisdom* and *Wit and Science*, invites the
audience to see her deformed face as a sign of her corrupt soul. Linking her
deformity to her murder of her husband, Sforza, Lucretia announces that
her facial "spots" are moral "blots." Her dialogue further explicates and
elaborates the stage image by invoking the leprous Cressida: "Me thinkes I

see the liuely counterfet, / Of catiue [wretched] *Cressed* in her misery, / Ingenderd out of hir disloyalty. . ." (ll. 2123–2125). The emphasis in this scene on the face as symbolic of soul culminates in the final scene when the devil *"ceazeth* [seizes] *on"* Alexander's *"face"* to indicate, by a forceful stage action, his possession of the Pope's soul (V.vi.3212). Lucretia's tincture scene is a clear example of how a stage image that is based on face-painting conventions can be employed to elucidate and reinforce the general theme of the play. Facial disfiguration provides a "speaking shew" for spiritual damnation.

A more static and simpler way of using face-painting as a dramatic image can be seen in Thomas Dekker's *The Whore of Babylon*. The play is close to the morality models in its obvious allegory. Two back-to-back scenes exhibit the difference between Truth, serving Titania the Fairie Queene, "vnder whom is figured our late Queene Elizabeth," and "Falshood," serving the Empress of Babylon, "vnder whom is figured *Rome*." [19] The dialogue between Plaine-Dealing and Truth in III.iii. explicates the picture which the audience sees in the next scene. Paint and spots, particularly pockmarks, we are told, are signs of falsehood and physical and spiritual sickness:

PLAIN.

But how shall I know, thou art the right truth?

TRUTH.

Because I am not painted.

(ll. 1–2)

TRUTH.

my Skins not spotted

With foule disease, as is that common harlot,

That baseborne trueth, that liues in *Babylon*.

PLAIN.

Why? is shee spotted?

TRUTH.

All ouer, with strange vglines, all ouer.

PLAIN.

Then she has got the pox . . . .

(ll. 10–15)

19. *The Dramatic Works of Thomas Dekker*, ed. Fredson Bowers (Cambridge, Eng., 1955), "DRAMMATIS PERSONAE," II, 496.

In the dumb show at the beginning of the following scene, "Falshood" appears "*(attir'd as* Truth *is) her face spotted*" (IV.i.). Standing "*aloofe behold-ing all*," Plaine-Dealing, Time, and Truth interpret the stage image. The obvious "small poxe" of "this freckled face queane" (ll. 57–58) who "hast collour enough in [her] face already" (l. 48), are pointed to as signs of fraud and corruption. Like Plaine-Dealing, who was previously "be-witched" by Falsehood who "was then in [his] eye, the goodliest woman that euer wore fore part of Sattin" (ll. 61–63), the audience is instructed to see that the colored face of Falsehood signals deceit. Falsehood's paint counterfeits Truth's beauty and proclaims visually what Time declares verbally at the beginning of the scene: Falsehood "calles forth men / To their destruction" (ll. 2–3).

To turn from lesser-known dramas to one of the better-known plays of the period, we see that Marlowe's *Dr. Faustus* offers a more complex juxtaposition of plain truth and painted falsehood.[20] Here the emphasis is on how Faustus's failure to see painted falsehood leads to his destruction. Faustus's moral blindness is expressed in stage images that depend on the white-devil convention. Marlowe counts on the audience's recognition of this convention and Faustus's willful blindness to it. In a series of stage images he opposes the true ugliness of the devil (the obvious black devil) to the deceptively painted appeal of the white devil. Like Lucifer in *Wisdom*, the devils in *Dr. Faustus* change their ugliness "into bryghtnes" in order "to-begyle" their victim. When Faustus first conjures the devil, he recoils at the ugly shape that appears before him:

---

20. In the most famous of Renaissance plays where the emphasis on truth, falsehood, and "seeming" is greatest, as Maynard Mack has pointed out in "The World of Hamlet," *The Yale Review*, XLI (1952), 502–523, we would expect to find face-painting used to underline the theme of deception, as we do in the lines of Polonius (III.i.43–48), Claudius (III.i.48–52), and Hamlet (III.i.142–144; III.iv.40–45; V.i.192–195), *Hamlet*, The Riverside Shakespeare, ed. G. Blakemore Evans (Boston, 1974). Howard Felperin in *Shakespearean Representation: Mimesis and Modernity in Elizabethan Tragedy* (Princeton, N.J., 1977), links both Hamlet with his twin pictures and Vindice with his skull and with his "indictments of cosmetic art" to the preaching Virtues of the morality tradition who use a visual aid to bring home a moral point (pp. 163–164); and he relates Gertrude's recogni-tion of "black and grained spots" in her soul to the literal representation of the spotted Anima in *Wisdom* (pp. 50–52). To enforce visually Gertrude's corruption, the "tinct" of her moral spots might appear in her face as well as in her soul.

> I charge thee to return and change thy shape,
> Thou art too ugly to attend on me.
> Go, and return an old Franciscan friar:
> That holy shape becomes a devil best.[21]

(I.iii.23–26)

Similarly, Faustus refuses the repellent "woman devil" at the sight of which he recoils, yet he embraces Helen, the "white devil" who, like "Mistress Minx"—Lechery of the Seven Deadly Sins—would wear face-paint[22] to signify both her role as a tempting paramour and her function as a white devil disguising her true ugliness. Faustus's famous question, "Was this the face that launch'd a thousand ships / And burnt the topless towers of Ilium?" (V.i.92–93), is an ironic pointing to a potent image of destruction whose significance Faustus chooses to ignore. Although he interprets the image rightly when he says "Her lips suck forth my soul" (l. 95), he chooses to postpone the moral consequence of his choice, just as he does in his dealings with Mephostophilis. Faustus's pointing to Helen's painted face is a powerful example of how an image that depends on the white-devil convention sums up the theme of willful blindness to evil.

Sejanus and *Catiline* illustrate another way face-painting functions on stage. Jonson uses the act of face-painting itself to exemplify visually the central theme of assuming false faces. Eudemus paints Livia's face with scarlet and white to "Make a light *fucus*" (cosmetic paint) while he advises her how to poison her husband and how to apply "an excellent new *fucus*."[23] Applying face-paint symbolically acts out the play's concern with deceit—with "shift of faces" (I.7). In Act V "*Fortune* auerts her face" from Sejanus (l. 186) and Tiberius, "(Acting his *tragedies* with a *comick* face)"

21. *The Tragical History Of The Life And Death Of Doctor Faustus*, in *The Plays of Christopher Marlowe*, ed. Leo Kirschbaum (Cleveland, 1962).

22. I agree with Kirschbaum's observation that "Lechery is a highly made-up woman" (p. 125).

23. *Sejanus*, in *Ben Jonson*, ed. C. H. Herford and Percy and Evelyn Simpson, 11 vols. (Oxford, 1925–1952), vol. IV, II.62 ff. For Jonson's condemnation of cosmetic whiteners like "Turners oyle of Talck," see his poem, "*An Epigram. To the small Poxe*," *The Vnderwood*, XXXIV, in *Ben Jonson*, vol. VIII. On the common meaning of "fucus" as "deceit," see the dedicatory poem in Thomas Tuke's *A Treatise Against Paint{i}ng* (London, 1616), B1ᵛ.

(IV.379), sends a masterpiece of deceitful rhetoric to the senators which cunningly announces his change of affection from Sejanus to Macro and which precipitates Sejanus's fall. In Act II of *Catiline* cosmetic application on stage also provides a symbolic visual show of fraud. The dialogue between the ladies, which juxtaposes dissection of politicians to critiques of tooth powder and face paints, invites the audience to see the cosmetic "cover up" being acted out as an image of the political deception that pervades the play.[24]

Webster's *The White Devil* shows most strikingly how face-painting universalizes a theme and extends its meaning through a wide range of characters. The convention of the black-faced devil disguising his face with white paint is crucial not only to Webster's title but also to his theme, the existence of "degrees of evils" and "degrees of devils"[25] at all levels of society. The many verbal references to devilishly black sin and lust and deceptively white surfaces are visually expressed in the black and white faces of Vittoria, Brachiano, Francisco, and Zanche which are used as powerful stage images of social, political, and sexual corruption.

For a flamboyant instance where the audience is directed to see a made-up face as a picture of moral and sexual corruption, consider the arraignment of Vittoria where Monticelso intends to exhibit "the proofs / Of [Vittoria's] black lust" to make her and Brachiano "infamous" (III.i.6–7). Like the morality preacher, Wisdom, first the lawyer and then Monticelso ask us to behold corruption: *"Domine judex converte oculos in hanc pestem mulierum corruptissimam"* (III.ii.10–11). Monticelso calls attention to the red and white face-paint that symbolizes what the lawyer's Latin terms Vittoria's taint and corruption:

> I shall be plainer with you, and paint out
> Your follies in more natural red and white
> Than that upon your cheek.
>
> (ll. 51–53)

---

24. For a fuller discussion of Jonson's distinctive use of the cosmetic or fucus scene in six of his plays, see my "Face-Painting Scenes in Ben Jonson's Plays," *SP*, LXXVII (1980), 388–401.

25. Ed. J. R. Mulryne (Lincoln, Neb., 1969), IV.ii.56–57.

Pointing to "This devil" and "This whore," Monticelso expatiates on the "devils" adultery and murder and identifies Vittoria with the white devil who, as Lucifer says in *Wisdom*, changes "into bryghtnes" in order "to-begyle" mankind:

> If the devil
> Did ever take good shape, behold his picture.
> (ll. 216–217)

But Vittoria is no mere Anima, and her trial is not a simple arraignment of corrupted mankind. With a more sophisticated vision of devils and of hypocrisy than the author of *Wisdom*, Webster builds upon the convention by having Vittoria respond in kind in accusing Monticelso of being a "devil" (l. 280) and by dramatizing here and elsewhere in the play the existence of more terrifying and deadlier white and black devils than Vittoria. Brachiano is in turn deceived by the white devil Florence into mistakenly cursing Vittoria's "beauty" and exclaiming, "How long have I beheld the devil in crystal?" (IV.ii.84). As Flamineo perceptively remarks,

> As in this world there are degrees of evils,
> So in this world there are degrees of devils.
> (ll. 56–57)

Although Vittoria is the most pointed-at white devil in the play, Webster indicates, by the use of face-paint, that she has a mighty opposite when Francisco, Duke of Florence, appears in Act V disguised as the black-faced moor Mulinassar to confirm his plot to have Brachiano "given up to the devil" (V.iii.151) and to have Vittoria, Flamineo, and Zanche put to death. The spectacle of the black-faced Francisco, the man who sent Brachiano's poison, standing by his dying victim and pretending to offer him words "of comfort" (l. 28) creates a powerful image of moral and political corruption.

Both Brachiano's and Zanche's faces are also speaking pictures. Brachiano's physical and spiritual death is to be seen in his face, poisoned with "devilish pothecary stuff" (V.iii.159). Francisco's remark that "There's death in's face already" (l. 80) alerts us to more than signs of mere mortality. The visible facial blotches and deformities caused by the mercury and quicksilver, like the physical deformities in the morality plays, provide a visible sign that Brachiano, guilty of murder and adultery, is indeed, as Lodovico exclaims, a "cursed devil" (l. 165) who is "damn'd" (l. 148) and "given up to the devil" (l. 151). Zanche's black face signals her sexual corruption, her devilish lust and trickery. Repeatedly pointed to as "this devil" (V.i.84), "the infernal" (V.iii.213), and "a strumpet" (V.i.182), Zanche is identified with the disguised Francisco, her "countryman, a goodly person" (V.i.92), whom she pursues with lust, as she did Flamineo:

> I ne'er lov'd my complexion till now,
> 'Cause I may boldly say without a blush
> I love you.
>
> (V.i.206–208)

To pursue the object of her lust, she betrays her mistress and reveals to the disguised Francisco and Lodovico the murder of Isabella and Camillo. Her suggestion that the "hundred thousand crowns" dowry which she intends to steal from Vittoria will "wash the Ethiop white" (V.iii.259) points ironically to the play's theme and to her own attempt to disguise her immorality. These black and white faces are used as forceful stage images to express a wide range of moral corruption and to make striking visual distinctions between "degrees of devils."

 The Duchess of Malfi provides another example of how Webster deepens the significance of face-painting images and uses them to express a range of thematic material. When the Old Lady (midwife to the Duchess) enters in II.i., Bosola points to her "scurvy face-physic"[26] as a sign of courtly hypocrisy. Her function in this scene is clearly to provide a visual cue for Bosola to interpret. Using the image of the Old Lady "come from painting" (l. 21) as the focal point of his lecture, Bosola equates her vile cosmetic arts with all levels of courtly deception, ranging from Castruchio's simple-minded face-making to the richly decked "outward form of man" which hides his "deformity," his "rotten and dead" body "eaten up of lice and worms" and "diseases" (ll. 45 ff.), to the Duchess's loose-bodied gown which

26. Ed. John Russell Brown (London, 1964), II.i.23.

Bosola suspects of hiding her pregnancy. The image of the painted Old Lady is used to exemplify what Ferdinand in I.i.309 and 313 terms the "Hypocrisy" of those "whose faces do belie their hearts."

In III.ii. Webster manipulates a conventional face-painting scene to clarify his own dramatic purposes. Here Webster alters the convention to convey a more complex vision of morality. The scene begins with the Duchess's call, "Bring me the casket hither, and the glass" (l. 1), a call which in *Catiline* (II.1–2), *The Devil's Charter* (IV.iii.2014 ff.), and in other plays signals the makeup and vanity scene preceding an assignation. [27] There is jesting talk of "face-making" (l. 52) and of changing hair "colour" with orris powder as the Duchess's hair is brushed. But like the play itself, this cosmetic vanity scene builds on certain expectations about a lustful, sensual widow only to surprise us with a variation and complication of the pattern. The "lover" the Duchess meets is her overly fond brother who presents her with a poniard; and the "lusty widow" whom Ferdinand brands "a notorious strumpet" (II.v.4) shows a spirit too great to be confined by conventional patterns. Webster alters the convention to express the moral ambiguity of his Duchess, the mixture of lusty widow and loving wife whose nature far transcends that of Painter's merely lustful and hypocritical prototype. [28]

The most macabre instances of face-painting are the scenes that link poison and painting in *The Revenger's Tragedy*, *The Second Maiden's Tragedy*, and *The Duke of Milan*. The painting scenes in the last two plays have proved especially troubling. Commenting on *The Duke of Milan*, T. A. Dunn finds that "The last scene, adapted rather than imitated from Act V, scene ii, of *The Second Maiden's Tragedy* with its disguises, the painting of the dead Marcelia's face to give an appearance of life, and the device of the poisoned lips, makes a finale which, quite apart from any question of the

27. An extended example is Thomas Dekker, *The Honest Whore, Part I*, in *The Dramatic Works of Thomas Dekker*, ed. Fredson Bowers, vol. II (Cambridge, Eng., 1955), II.i.1 ff. and stage directions.

28. Painter's black and white portrait is of a Duchess who made "hir waie to pleasure, which she lusted more than marriage, the same seruing hir, but for a Maske and couerture to hide her follies and shamlesse lusts, for which she did the penance that hir follie deserued," Appendix I, extract from *The Palace of Pleasure*, in John Russell Brown, ed., *The Duchess of Malfi*, pp. 184–185.

mere plotting, is to the modern reader ludicrously melodramatic" and "bathetic." [29] Similarly, S. Schoenbaum terms the main plot of *The Second Maiden's Tragedy* and the cosmetic poisoning scene "lurid and fantastic." [30] Robert Ornstein dismisses "the frequently preposterous *Second Maiden's Tragedy*" in a footnote because, among other reasons, "it contributes little or nothing to the sum of Jacobean tragedy." [31]

To appreciate how these cosmetic poisoning scenes function as dramatic rhetoric, we need first to see them in the context of Renaissance ideas about poison and paint. In fact, cosmetics did contain poison, so the stage actions present an extension of reality, not merely preposterous fantasy. The main ingredient of most face-whiteners, rouges, and lip salves was ceruse (from the Latin *cerussa* or white lead), which was made by exposing plates of lead to the vapor of vinegar. When coloring was added—such as red ocher or red crystalline mercuric sulphide, called vermilion—ceruse became "paint" for cheeks and lips. [32] Moralists like Tuke pointed out that "the vse of this ceruse, besides the rotting of the teeth, and the vnsauourie breath which it causeth, being ministred in paintings, doth turne faire creatures into infernall Furies" (B4[v]). Warning women about the effects of ceruse, Richard Haydocke observes that "those women which vse it about their faces, doe quickly become withered and gray headed, because this doth so mightely drie vp the naturall moysture of their flesh." [33] Ceruse was classified as a poison in the *De Venenis* of Petrus Abbonus and in Ambroise Paré's *Workes*, translated by Thomas Johnson in 1634. The warnings of physicians and moralists against ceruse are corroborated by Paré's remark that ceruse is a "dry poyson" which "make[s] the tongue and

29. T. A. Dunn, *Philip Massinger: The Man and the Playwright* (London, 1957), p. 68.

30. *Middleton's Tragedies: A Critical Study* (New York, 1955), p. 51.

31. *The Moral Vision of Jacobean Tragedy* (Madison, Wis., 1960), p. 289, n. 1.

32. See Williams, *Powder and Paint,* p. 15; Camden, *The Elizabethan Woman,* pp. 178, 180; "De Venenis of Petrus Abbonus," trans. Horace M. Brown, *Annals of Medical History,* VI (1924), 31.

33. Trans., "A DISCOVRSE OF THE ARTIFICIALL beauty of women," Book III of *A Tracte Containing the Artes of Curious Paintinge Caruinge & Building,* Giovanni Lomazzo (Oxford, 1598), p. 130.

throate dry and rough" and by Petrus Abbonus's observation that it causes "blackened teeth."[34]

Sublimate of mercury was another common skin whitener and also a readily available poison. Women frequently used sublimate of mercury and ceruse as skin-peelers to remove smallpox scars and other blemishes. In fact, removing spots was a recurring problem with both women and men, to judge from the variety of complaints and remedies in Sir Hugh Platt's popular *Delightes for Ladies*.[35] Paré reports that the poison, cantharides, was used as a skin bleach to cure a woman's severe facial blotches (p. 800). Barnabe Barnes tried to poison John Browne with mercury sublimate which he had purchased at a grocer's.[36] What helped to make Frances Howard's face white helped to kill her victim, Sir Thomas Overbury, who was poisoned in the tower by her agents. Paré notes that sublimate has "a corroding and putrefying quality" (p. 778) and that among other things it causes a swollen tongue and internal and external corrosion or burning (p. 810). Tuke quotes "The Inuectiue of Doctore Andreas de Laguna, . . . against the painting of women" on "The excellencie of this Mercurie sublimate": "women, who often paint themselues with it, though they be very young, they presently turne old with withered and wrinkled faces like an Ape, and before age come vpon them, they tremble (poore wretches) as if they were sicke of the staggers, reeling, and full of quick-siluer, for so are they" (B4ʳ). Renaissance dramatists exploited what Paré describes as one of *"The generall signes of such as are poysoned,"* which is that "the colour of the face changeth suddenly, somewhiles to blacke, sometimes to yellow, or any other colour, much differing from the common custome of man" (p. 778). What happened to women's faces when they used sublimate of mercury is a milder version of the blackened or blotched face and corroded teeth and tongue which Lucretia,

34. "OF POYSONS," Book 21 in Ambroise Paré, *Workes*, trans. Thomas Johnson (London, 1634), p. 779; "De Venenis of Petrus Abbonus," p. 40, notes that blackened teeth are one of the symptoms of ceruse poisoning.

35. One such recipe for "a good skinning salue" consists of "Brimstone ground with the oile of Turpentine" and butter (p. 94).

36. Fredson T. Bowers, "The Audience and the Poisoners of Elizabethan Tragedy," *JEGP*, XXXVI (1937), 503; Mark Eccles, "Barnabe Barnes," in *Thomas Lodge and Other Elizabethans*, ed. Charles J. Sisson (Cambridge, Mass., 1933), pp. 177–179, 182, 190.

Brachiano, and other victims suffer when poisoned. This linking of cosmet-ics and poison is evident in Vives's popular work on the education of women:

The tender skynne wyl reuyll the more sone, and all the fauour of the face waxeth olde, and the breth stynketh, and the tethe rusten, and an yuell ayre all the bodye ouer, bothe by the reason of the ceruse, and quick siluer, and specially by the reason of the soopes, wherwith theye prepare the bodye, as it were a table, ayenste the peyntynge on the nexte day. Wherfore Ouyde called these doynges venomes, and not without a cause.[37]

The increasing use of poisoned cosmetics in Jacobean tragedies also reflects the period's fascination with Italy as the center of both poisoning and cosmetics (the best ceruse came from Italy), as well as actual poisoning attempts like that on Overbury and the bizarre attempts to poison Queen Elizabeth and the Earl of Essex by anointing the pommel of her saddle and the arms of his chair. Poisoning was considered the most detestable form of murder,[38] and the instances of poisoning in tragedy indicate the period's taste for sensationalism. The self-conscious mockery of face-paint-ing evident in the comments of both Vindice and Francisco suggests a more sophisticated and satiric awareness of both conventions and actual practices on the part of the audience. When in *The Duke of Milan* Francisco says to the dead Marcelia, "Your ladyship looks pale, / But I, your doctor, have a ceruse for you," he counts on a "knowing" audience as he does when he mocks the sour-smelling breaths of court ladies while he paints Marcelia's lips with poison.[39]

When placed in this context of Renaissance notions of poison and paint, the cosmetic poisoning scenes can be seen as central dramatic images that use face-painting conventions to create spectacular didactic shows. In particular, the poisoned kiss is a dramatic vehicle for the transference of

37. *Instruction of a Christen Woman*, trans. Richard Hyrde (London, 1541), G.iii.ᵛ.
38. Bowers, p. 497.
39. *The Selected Plays of Philip Massinger*, ed. Colin Gibson (Cambridge, Eng., 1978), V.ii. 183–184. One connection a "knowing" audience might make is between sour breath and venereal disease. Discussing "quick-silver," Paré notes that it is used in ointments or plasters to treat venereal disease and that "besides, it causeth the breath of such as are anointed therewith to stinke" (p. 811).

poison as well as a significant action that draws the audience's attention to sexual corruption. *Marie Magadalene* provides a morality play precedent for the use of kissing to represent devilish seduction. Mary's kissing of the Vices is repeatedly pointed to as a "token" or sign of their power over her.[40] So, too, when Faustus kisses the painted white devil Helen, his exclamation that "Her lips suck forth my soul" (V.i.95) underlines what is being acted out. William Prynne's condemnation in his *Histriomastix*, "the scourge of players," of *"those venemous unchaste, incestuous kisses"* whose *"poysonous filthinesse"* he takes pains to anatomize,[41] provides the moralists' gloss for the poisoned kiss on stage.

In *The Revenger's Tragedy* the "bony lady" scene epitomizes the false shows of the court and acts out the pattern of seduction and destruction by lust which dominates the play. The pattern is established in the beginning scene which details the Duke's poisonous lust; it is continued in the rape by the Duchess's Youngest Son of Antonio's wife (which leads to his death) and in Spurio's liaison with the Duchess; and it culminates in Act V in the murders committed by the falsely masked revengers. Vindice's painted, poisoned skull provides a striking visual realization of the many "false forms" and disguised sins in the play. Sin is repeatedly spoken of in cosmetic terms or imaged in the face or forehead. The rape of Antonio's wife has "Thrown ink upon the forehead of our state."[42] Vindice, chastising Gratiana, who apostrophizes the heavens to "Take this infectious spot out of my soul" (IV.iv.52), tells her, "do but imagine, / Now the disease has left you, how leprously / That office would have cling'd unto your forehead" (ll. 62–64). Lussurioso speaks of "offences / Gilt o'er with mercy" which "show like fairest women, / Good only for their beauties, which wash'd off, / No sin is uglier" (I.ii.28–31). In the haste which Ambitioso and Supervacuo show to have Lussurioso executed, the Duke sees "envy with a poor thin cover o'er't" (II.iii.105).[43] As he is about to kiss the supposedly "bashful country lady," the Duke voices the deceitful courtly ethic:

40. See ll. 478–481, 491–494, 724–727, 795–799.

41. (New York, 1974), p. 166. Prynne also condemns "the common *accursed hellish art of face-painting*" as the epitome of how stage-plays pervert God's works *"in putting a false glosse upon his creatures"* (pp. 159–160).

42. Ed. Lawrence J. Ross (Lincoln, Nebr., 1966), I.ii.4.

43. See also I.i.20–22, I.iv.28–30, III.vi.37–38, V.i.22–23, 170–171.

> In gravest looks the greatest faults seem less;
> Give me that sin that's rob'd in holiness.
>
> (III.v.137–138)

By kissing what is an epitome of "false forms," the Duke acts out the central idea that sinful lust beguiles with fair surfaces, "superfluous outsides," which hide deadly corruption. Vindice's cry of "Royal villain! white devil!" (l. 144) elaborates what is being acted out: the devil beguiled, the cheater cheated.

In *The Second Maiden's Tragedy* the explicit verbal and visual emphasis on face underlines the fatal attraction of "face" or lust which is acted out in both plots by chaste/illicit kisses. In both the main plot with the Tyrant, the Lady, and Govianus, and the subplot, with the illicit relation between the Wife (a Lady Lechery type) and Votarius, lust is symbolized repeatedly by the word "face." Doubling the parts of the Wife and the Lady (Chastity), as Anne Lancashire suggests,[44] would enforce the moral point and the link between the two plots. Both the Tyrant and Votarius die poisoned by lust—by the attraction of a "face." In the subplot, the seductive Wife is repeatedly regarded as a visual object and identified with "face": "O, who could move / Adultery to yon face!" (I.ii.73–74); "I'll see your face no more" (l. 238); "Face, fare thee well" (l. 257); "He's too familiar with the face I love" (II.ii.94). In Act V the Tyrant forces Govianus, disguised as a painter, to "hide death upon" the Lady's "face" (V.ii.81) and to "force beauty on" her "face" (l. 110). To effect his revenge, Govianus applies poisoned face-paint, symbolizing the poison of lust. The recurring stage action of chaste/unchaste kissing links the plots and gives visual expression to the theme. The chaste, loving initial kiss which the Lady gives Govianus in I.i.164 has its opposite visual analogue in the adulterous kiss which Votarius gives the Wife in I.ii.250 ff. when we see him "kiss destruction" (l. 248).[45] These visual images culminate in V.ii. when the Tyrant dies after kissing the poisoned lips of the Lady.

Middleton's *Women Beware Women* also uses a poisoned kiss and a dis-

---

44. Anne Lancashire, ed., *The Second Maiden's Tragedy* (Manchester, 1978), p. 55.
45. See also I.ii.315, II.ii.47–51, III.iii.248–251, IV.i.33–34, 104–105, 166.

figured face to act out the effects of the "sin" of "lust."[46] In I.i.54 we are asked to "View but [Bianca's] face" to "see all her dowry" of beauty and virtue. In V.ii. her face is again the index of her nature, now corrupted. After she kisses the Duke whom she has mistakenly poisoned, she calls attention to her disfigured face caused by the poison: "But my deformity in spirit's more foul— / A blemished face best fits a leprous soul" (ll. 204–205).

As final proof for my argument that face-painting provides a repeated crucial focus for theme and image in Renaissance tragedy, consider the face-painting scene in Massinger's *The Duke of Milan*. This scene, which is generally recognized as being adapted from *The Second Maiden's Tragedy*,[47] has troubled modern readers like T. A. Dunn who finds it "ludicrously melodramatic" and writes that it "appears all the more bathetic after the subtlety of the earlier scenes (e.g., Act II, scene i) between Marcelia and Francisco" (p. 68). In fact, it is precisely this earlier "subtle" scene (II.i) that establishes Francisco's role as devilish tempter and that provides a significant visual analogue to the "bathetic" kiss in V.ii. When Marcelia swoons in II.i. after reading her supposed death warrant from her husband which Francisco has given her, a regretful Francisco desperately tries to "kiss her into a new life" (l. 382) just as the despairing Sforza will try in Act V to kiss life into her dead body. Francisco's lustful kissing of Marcelia in II.i.287 provides a visual parallel to Sforza's passionate kissing of his wife in I.iii.68–69 and in III.iii.113. Sforza's jealous concern that Marcelia's "sweet lips, yielding immortal nectar" might "Be gently touch'd by any but [himself]" (I.iii.205–206) establishes the symbolic link between lips and kissing and lust. His repetition of "sweetness" and "nectar" as he is about to kiss Marcelia's poisoned lips in V.ii. echoes the earlier passage. Thus Francisco's application to Marcelia's lips of a poisoned "precious antidote old ladies use / When they would kiss, knowing their gums are rotten" (V.ii.190–191) is not an isolated piece of sensationalism but in fact serves as the focal point of patterns established in

46. Ed. J. R. Mulryne (Manchester, 1975). V.ii.222, 225, III.iii.11 ff., and III.ii. 136–142 describe lust in terms of face-painting. The commendatory verses link whores, poison, and lust: "drabs of state, vexed, / Have plots, poisons, mischiefs that seldom miss, / To murder virtue with a venom kiss" (ll. 2–4).

47. See Lancashire, p. 56, and Dunn, p. 68.

the earlier scenes. Earlier scenes also set up the opposition between Marcelia's "clear and untainted" and "unspotted" beauty and painted courtly corruption which culminates in Francisco's painting Marcelia's face with ceruse and poisoned lip salve—visually transforming her into an emblem of courtly deceit and corrupted lust to trap the Duke. By kissing the painted and poisoned face of the woman he has murdered because of jealous lust, the Duke presents a climactic "speaking shew" of how blind lust destroys.

The closing lines of *The Duke of Milan*, which refer back to the painting and poisoning the audience has just witnessed, summarize a central theme in all three of these plays: "learn from this example, there's no trust / In a foundation that is built on lust" (V.ii.268–269). In all three plays the dead face or skull of an innocent woman is painted with poisoned colors, and the revenger-painter points to the face as a picture of courtly hypocrisy, of "white devils," and of the deceitful and deadly temptation of lust—imaged in the false and poisonous colors of the painted face. In each play the audience watches a lustful victim in the act of being attracted and trapped by this deceiving painted face. In a display of "convention in action," the victim kisses the poisoned lips and dies, acting out the idea that painted lust leads to a spiritual and physical death. In each case a central scene builds upon the kind of stage image found in other plays and on the widespread cosmetic associations of the period.

From Anima's disfigured and Wit's shamefully black and spotted face to Marcelia's colored and poisoned face is a long journey but a revealing one. In each play the dramatist draws upon conventions of the disfigured or painted face to create striking stage images or symbolic shows. In simpler plays these visual images express physical and spiritual deformity. In more sophisticated Renaissance tragedies, dramatists use face-painting to express a wide range of social, political, and sexual corruption. To overlook the many recurring painted faces in these plays or to dismiss their heightened and sometimes poisoned colors as preposterous is to miss a major element of Renaissance dramatic art.

Shakespeare's Oral Text

MARION TROUSDALE

T HE QUESTION as to whether Shakespeare's plays exist only in perfor-
mance is one I considered in an earlier volume of *Renaissance Drama*. [1]
I return to it here in order to look more closely at the ways in which
Shakespeare the Playwright is necessarily Shakespeare the Poet. G. E.
Bentley has argued that those studies of imagery which grew under the
reign of the new critics assume a reader rather than a spectator of the plays.
The evidence shows that during the course of his career Shakespeare had no
interest in the readers of his plays. Bentley argues from this that on
historical grounds such studies of imagery must be deemed invalid. That
is, he assumes that such things as figures of speech, iterative images,
dominant metaphors, poetic symbols, though they may be generated by
an artist such as Milton in his study at Horton, are not oral concerns. [2] My
argument here is that they are. Bentley chastises the modern critic who in
pursuit of Shakespeare's themes fails to consider Shakespeare's work "in the
historical environment in which his creative genius operated." But a
broader consideration of that historical environment suggests the need for
a different sense of the oral. What I wish to examine here is the nature of
oral convention. Such an examination raises a more fundamental question
as to the nature of language. In what ways does language meant to be
spoken differ from language meant to be read? And ought we to assume
that that difference in the sixteenth century would be the same as it may be
today? I shall begin with an early masque of Gascoigne as a means of

1. N.S. IV (1971), 3–36.
2. "Shakespeare and the Readers of His Plays," *Shakespeare and His Theatre* (Lincoln,
Nebr., 1964), pp. 1–26.

95

illustrating the nature of the problem. I want then to look at some of the conventions by means of which Shakespeare develops themes and uses erudite sources and spins imagistic patterns. They are conventions, I feel, that originate not in a critic's study but in the requirements of performance. Memory is crucial to any kind of meaningful perception. In an oral art memory is dependent on the ear.

I

Preparations for the masque to celebrate the joint marriage of the son and daughter of Anthony Browne, the Viscount of Montague, to the daughter and son of Sir William Dormer were already well advanced when George Gascoigne's help was sought in the autumn of 1572.[3] The eight masquers had "brought furniture of silks, etc.," we are told, "and had caused their garments to be cut of the Venetian fashion." But they then "began to imagine that (without some speciall demonstracion) it would seeme somewhat obscure to haue Venetians presented rather than other countrey men." To repair this incongruity, they begged Gascoigne to devise some "discourse conuenient to render a good cause of the Venetians presence."[4] Gascoigne seems to have done at least that. The boy actor who subsequently introduced the masque, claiming to be a Mounthermer by his father's side and a Mounatucute [Montague] by his mother's, told the assembled guests how his father was slain at the siege of Famagusta and he himself as captive to the Turks made witness to the Battle of Lepanto, to be rescued finally not only by Venetians but by members of the Venetian Montagues whose boat, blown off course by a tempest, ended up fortuitously by the English coast and thereafter found its way down the Thames, just so the Italian Montagues with the English boy might join in the family marriage celebrations.

The tale is told in a lugubrious poulter's measure with the marks of that early self-conscious art that for some make Shakespeare's humanist debt so hard to accept.

3. C. T. Prouty, *George Gascoigne: Elizabethan Courtier, Soldier, and Poet* (New York, 1942), pp. 57–62, 173–177. George Gascoigne, *A Hundred Sundry Flowers* (1573; rpt. Menston, Eng., 1970), pp. 382–383.

4. Gascoigne, *Sundry Flowers*, p. 382.

And you shall know the cause, wherefore these robes are worne,
And why I go outlandishlike, yet being english borne,
And why I thus presume to press into this place,
And why I (simple boy) am bold to looke such men in face.[5]

One might remark on the irregular meter and the too insistent rhyme. One is just as apt to sigh under the weight and verbal battering of the anaphora. The importance of such early verse in considering the differences of language meant to be spoken and language meant to be read is as much its occasion as its technique. As I look at it I see it on the page as a written and indeed a printed text. But it was composed for oral delivery as part of a social occasion. If we were to accept Bentley's strictures, the conditions under which I study it as text are themselves conditions in which the language as utterance might appear in a different if not necessarily less favorable light. I look upon this verse in that context as representative of dramatic verse generally. In what ways might we claim what we read as text to be utterance, and does it change the nature of the text if we do so? We know that this particular poem was written for oral delivery, but we need not hear it in order to understand it, and with that rhythm and that rhyme, we might say, it may have been spoken, but it is hardly speech. What we can say about it at this point is that it exists as something oral that is written, a kind of oxymoron whose contradiction I want to compound by attaching to it a contradictory label, that of an oral text.

Both *oral* and *text* form the skeleton of the argument that follows, and I feel it important to explain as precisely as I can what I mean when I use those two words. The distinction between them is basically that which is often made between that which is spoken and that which is written. Such a distinction seems obvious enough, but because there is often hidden in it fundamental beliefs about the nature of language, the two modes of discourse have always attracted partisans, most of them on the side of the spoken word. Socrates says in *Phaedrus* that a man who has knowledge of the just, the beautiful, the good will not "sow his seed" in ink by penning words which are unable to defend themselves by argument. Rather he will pursue the art of dialectic, an art which requires both the human voice and an active intellect.[6] Ernest Kapp, following this line of thought, has

5. *Ibid.*, p. 383.
6. *The Dialogues of Plato*, trans. B. Jowett (Oxford, 1892), I, 275–276.

shown how Aristotle's logic, in fact, developed out of the spoken word.[7] The Elizabethans, in their grammars at least, took for granted that language was speech. Grammar, Ben Jonson writes, "is the art of true, and well speaking a Language: the writing is but an Accident," that is, not essential to the nature of language.[8] More recently Walter Ong has argued that the invention of movable type changed the nature of our culture and the way in which we think. He describes that change as decay; like Rousseau much earlier he finds something vitiating about a text.[9] One suspects the same must be true of many Shakespeareans who argue with such feeling today that the plays are scripts which can be understood only when they are played. The strongest voice on the other side is that of Jacques Derrida who argues that if writing means in fact something which is sufficiently structured in its forms to be written, then writing, conceptually at least, precedes speech. It is only codification, what Derrida calls inscription, that makes it possible for words whose meanings are arbitrary to be used as a means of communication. Without such inscription, a word could mean a different thing each time that it was used.[10]

I see the definitions with which I wish to start as less partisan ones. I have taken them from the French philosopher Paul Ricoeur. He defines a text as every utterance or set of utterances fixed by writing, but adds that it is not simply a recording of prior speech. Rather "it invites directly in written words the meaning of the utterance." The distinction is made essentially in terms of reference. In speech, he points out, reference is linked to the situation—the speakers present, the cultural background, the perceptual surroundings. "Reference to reality" is "reference to that

7. *Greek Foundations of Traditional Logic* (New York, 1942).

8. *The English Grammar* [*Works*, 1640] (Menston, Eng., 1972), p. 35. The 1585 English version of *The Latine Grammar of P. Ramus* begins, "Grammar is the art to speak well" and defines a syllable as "a full or perfect sound in a word" (rpt. Amsterdam, 1971), pp. 1–2, 34. See also G. K. Hunter, *A Comparison of the Use of the Sententia, Considered as a Typical Rhetorical Ornament, in the Tragedies of Seneca, and in those of Gascoigne, Kyd, Heywood, Jonson, Marston, Dekker, Webster and Greville* (Thesis, Oxford University, 1950), pp. 26–45.

9. J. J. Rousseau, *Essai sur l'origine des langues*, ed. Charles Porset (Bordeaux; 1970). Walter Ong, *Ramus: Method and the Decay of Dialogue* (Cambridge, Mass., 1958).

10. Jacques Derrida, *Of Grammatology*, trans. Gayatri Chakrovorty Spivak (Baltimore, Md., 1976), pp. 44–46. Derrida is arguing against Ferdinand de Saussure's view that language is speech and that writing exists only in order to represent the spoken word.

reality which can be pointed out 'around' the speakers, 'around', so to speak, the instances of discourse itself." In a text, on the other hand, this reference is intercepted, which is to say that it is deferred or suspended. "As readers," he notes, "we can remain in the suspense of the text and treat it as a wordless and authorless text, in which case we explain it by means of its internal relations, its structure." If as readers we "prolong the suspension of referential relation," the text has no outside, only an inside. But we can also as readers through interpretation actualize the reference that is there. [11]

When we turn again to Gascoigne, we can see how such a masque is in one sense what Ricoeur recognizes as a form of speech. It was written for a particular situation, and reference to reality is "reference to that reality that can be pointed out around the speaker"—the Montagues, England, the joint wedding of Anthony Browne's two children. The actor not only directly addresses the wedding guests, but responds to their amazement at the unexpected appearance of the masquers. "What wonder you my Lords?" he asks, "Why gaze you gentlemen. And wherefore maruaile you mez Dames," and the whole tale, as we see by the earlier quoted anaphora, develops as an answer to the questions the audience is presumed to ask. It is at least half a conversation, and insofar as an audience is present, not an imagined one. And when he begins to answer those questions, his references are to such recent events as the siege of Famagusta and the battle of Lepanto—events, one assumes, the audience would know. [12]

There are other aspects of the text at its most formal which, if not exactly in the nature of conversation, directly concern an audience, and so, we might argue, are closer to speech than to text. At least they have behind them the assumptions of rhetoric, and their strategies are directed toward a live audience whom the speaker is expected to move. Thus the boy says of his rescue when the Venetian general struck off the Turkish captain's head:

11. Paul Ricoeur, "What Is a Text?" in David M. Rasmussen, ed., *Mythic-Symbolic Language and Philosophical Anthropology* (The Hague, 1971), pp. 135–140.

12. Famagusta fell on 15 August 1571. The Battle of Lepanto was fought on 7 October in the same year. The boy says, "As in October last vppon the seuenth day" (p. 388). Gascoigne, in fact, used a contemporary pamphlet as a source in his description of Famagusta. See Robert Ralston Cawley, "George Gascoigne and the Siege of Famagusta," *MLN*, XLIII (1928), 296–300.

> Oh howe I feele the bloud now tickle in my brest,
> To think what ioy then pierst my heart, and how I thought me blest
>
> (p.389)

The revelation of the boy's feelings is obviously meant to elicit sympathy from the Lords and Ladies as they imagine his plight. And when he describes the fate of the noble Bragadine after the siege of Famagusta whose ears were cut from his head and who was then "hoisted . . . alofte into the aire, / That so he might be shewed with crueltie and spight" (p. 387), he adds, "Unto vs all, whose weping eies did much abhorre the sight," giving immediacy to the tale he tells by description of his inward woe. Again this is obviously a speaking voice which as witness of a reported tale was meant to move a live audience.

At the same time we notice that this elaborate invention in its formal aspects—the rhyme, the meter, the too obvious figures—creates a structure that is essentially self-referring, one that seems closer in its nature to text. "For sure his hauty harte was bent, some great exployte to finde" has seven feet because the previous line had six, and it ends with *find* because the previous line ended with *mind*. Again the anaphora which we looked at earlier is made up formally of repetition of the first three words, and though it is meant to give emphasis to what follows by articulating the questions in the audience, it too as figure is self-referring. As we read it, it directs our attention inward as much as outward. What we "hear" is iteration, but as we mark the iteration silently we are not led, as we might be in listening to it, to assume as audience the questions that are asked. Self-referring as they are, however, and hence suggestive of text in one of Ricoeur's meanings, these same formal devices—the rhyme, the meter, the figures—are all oral devices whose effective use assumes not the eye but the ear. Even when we read the poem silently we do not *see* the repetition of the first three words of the anaphora—

> And why I go . . .
> And why I thus . . .
> And why I (simple boy) . . .

—we hear them, just as we hear the meter and the rhyme. Such formal devices are in their artistic intent aural, and in silent reading we often hear them with an inner ear.

There appears to be, then, as we examine Gascoigne's devices, a blurring of that boundary between the written and the oral that Ricoeur stakes out. All of the formal devices that we have noticed seem in origin and in intent to be oral devices. Reconsideration of such devices suggests that oral patterning which by definition must be governed by forms of repetition is necessarily self-referring and indeed must be self-referring to be coherent, even as a piece of music would lack cohesion if themes did not recur in different forms over and over again. If this is so, what Ricoeur defines as text because of its intrinsically formal structuring reflects in origin requirements which grew out of performance. A text in that context would not differ from an utterance except by virtue of the fact that it is written down.

I see Gascoigne in this instance as a latter-day oral poet. He has composed a verse for an oral occasion, and in it we see that both the verbal patterns and the larger structural orderings are governed by oral concerns. But he composed it, we assume, with the mnemonic aid of writing, and once he had composed it he sanctioned the printing of it that others might read what had originally been performed. [13] Thus printed, his masque became something more than performance, and its formal devices when no longer time governed became something other than a score. He seems in these circumstances to be an oral poet in a broader sense than that defined by occasion. I shall call him an oral poet principally because the verbal conventions which seem to control the smaller and larger verbal patterns of his composition are conventions which logically and historically attach themselves to the artistic and cultural concerns of an oral age. [14]

13. Though his name does not appear on the title page, it appears that Gascoigne was responsible for the first printing of *A Hundred Sundry Flowers*, in 1573. See C. T. Prouty, *George Gascoigne*, pp. 58–59, 78–80. The work was reissued, rearranged, and enlarged in 1575 under the title *The Posies*, and Gascoigne then put his name on the title page, publicly taking credit for the work.

14. The most important work on oral poetry has been done by Albert B. Lord, *The Singer of Tales* (Cambridge, Mass., 1960). See as well Ann Chalmers Watts, *The Lyre and the Harp* (New Haven, Conn., 1969); Ruth Finnegan, *Oral Poetry: Its Nature, Significance, and Social Context* (Cambridge, Eng., 1977); David Buchan, *The Ballad and the Folk* (London, 1972).

II

I shall make the same argument about Shakespeare. But before I examine what I feel to be some of the more important oral techniques in his plays, I want to look at one other earlier example, the famous and much parodied lament by Hieronimo in *The Spanish Tragedy*. I quote only the beginning, as the lines are well known.

> O eyes, no eyes, but fountains fraught with tears;
> O life, no life, but lively form of death;
> O world, no world, but mass of public wrongs,
> Confus'd and fill'd with murder and misdeeds.[15]

(III.ii. 1–4)

Hieronimo is alone on stage, and the soliloquy up until a letter "falleth" after line 23 gives us a plea for action on Hieronimo's part but does not otherwise advance the plot. It is there rather to engage the sympathy of the audience for Hieronimo. Its concerns are those of rhetoric.[16] We might at first think of his lines as utterance, if a very formal one. Interestingly, however, this famous opening into which Jonas Barish notes Kyd has packed three successive apostrophes achieving "an effect of swollen passion breaking loose,"[17] re-presents a scheme derived ultimately from Petrarch which more recently Sir Philip Sidney had used or was about to use.[18]

> O teares, no teares, but raine from beautie's skies,
>   Making those Lillies and those Roses grow,
>   Which ay most faire, now more then most faire show[19]

As Barish writes of the two: "In Sidney, the lady's manifestations of sorrow remain on the same level of importance and intensity; they do not evolve,

15. Ed. Philip Edwards (Cambridge, Mass., 1959).

16. G. K. Hunter, *A Comparison of the Use of the Sententia*, p. 23.

17. "The Spanish Tragedy, or The Pleasures and Perils of Rhetoric," *Elizabethan Theatre*, Stratford-upon-Avon Studies 9 (London, 1966), pp. 59–85. The quotation occurs on p. 76.

18. *Ibid.*, p. 76.

19. *Astrophil and Stella*, Sonnet 100, in William A. Ringler, Jr., ed., *The Poems of Sir Philip Sidney* (Oxford, 1962), p. 231.

except perhaps in the direction of increasing articulateness. Kyd proceeds climactically, through circles of widening significance: eyes, life, world, heavens—organ, organism, social milieu, cosmos. The theme is the progressive perversion of all order and health into disease and disorder through the murder of Horatio."[20] What we see in Hieronimo's lines, then, in addition to a highly structured expression of grief is a kind of textual citation, a recognition and exploitation of an earlier text. We know such citations to be common in Elizabethan dramatists. The device seems, if not pedantic, certainly excessively literary. Can we claim that this too is the device of an oral age?

The answer to that question is yes, and it suggests another aspect of the oral that I think we do not often consider. Jack Goody has recently argued that writing gives permanent form to speech. Words become enduring objects rather than evanescent aural signals, and language shifts from the aural to the visual. Logic, he claims, is a function of writing, for it is only the setting down of speech that enabled man clearly to separate words and manipulate their order.[21] But much of the evidence seems to be on the other side. It is the desire for accuracy and continuance that in part explains the invention of the printing press, but it is not the printing press that created that societal need. Prior to its existence other mnemonic devices had to be developed. Spoken language *is* ephemeral. But that which is ephemeral is not by virtue of that fact unstructured. Rather, language in an oral culture has of necessity to be highly codified if the culture itself is to survive. The poet must be able to compose without the aid of writing. In oral epic the voice perishes but the poem survives. It survives because the uses of language have been codified in such a way that without a written record the poem can be repeated, the aural can be made oral again. It is only by means of repetition that knowledge itself can continue and only by means of knowledge that a society can perpetuate itself. Cultural memory today is essentially the printed page; the ability to repeat depends upon inscription. The memory of an oral culture is similarly inscribed, but its inscriptions, which is to say its verbal memory, lie

20. "The Spanish Tragedy," pp. 76–77.
21. *The Domestication of the Savage Mind* (Cambridge, Eng., 1977).

in what we might call conventions, what Albert Lord describes as formulae. [22]

I am going to use that word *formula* in a very broad sense. Meter and
rhyme are obviously formulaic, a means of repeatability, a means of
memory both in the language itself and in the mind. Citation itself, we
might think, is even more important for the continuance of knowledge,
and it too is obviously formulaic. Kyd repeats certain phrases used by
Petrarch and Sidney. These are taken out of context and given another
sense. What is preserved is a way of saying something, a kind of language
code. We find a similar use of formulae in the period's addiction to
commonplaces. Such formulae are in a way like movable type. The same
letter can be used over and over again. But the value of its use lies in the
fact that it is movable. It was only when the same letter could be used in
different words that printing as we know it could begin.

Oral literature then, of necessity, requires a kind of inscription. What
the poet draws upon in order to compose is a storehouse of sound patterns,
figures, phrases, situations, themes. With these in hand he builds his
story; he builds it by ear, and he builds it cumulatively. He may condense,
elaborate, digress, and there is great freedom in the ways in which the
same story might be told. The story itself provides an ultimate destina-
tion. But the cohesiveness of the discrete scenes that one listens to is
created by the simple device of repetition, a device that is aural as well as
oral in its appeal to the ear. [23] The use of formulae rather than movable
type in the retelling means that the retelling is never the same.

---

22. *The Singer of Tales*, p. 96; G. S. Kirk, *Homer and the Oral Tradition* (Cambridge,
Eng., 1976), pp. 74–81. Lord, following Milman Parry, distinguishes formula from
theme. Formula is "a group of words which is regularly employed under the same metrical
conditions to express a given essential idea" within the songs of one singer (pp. 30, 43).
Themes are "groups of ideas regularly used in telling a tale" (p. 68). I am using the term
formula in this essay in a much broader sense to include repetition of recognized patterns of
both words and ideas.

23. Aural patterning appears to be very complex. See Buchan, *The Ballad and the Folk*,
pp. 87–165. I am indebted to Keith Brown for calling my attention to this source.

III

In what ways are such formulae reflected in the oral text of a Shakespearean play? I want first to look at what to me represent instances of formulae which recur within the canon. I mention only obvious repetitions here. They seem to me a kind of evidence that Shakespeare in fact composed in the way in which oral poets appear to have composed.[24] He reflects in his techniques as author the habits of an oral age. I shall then return to the question raised by Bentley by looking briefly at aural patterns within individual plays.

Probably the best-known instance of such compositional repetition is that of the plot of *Othello* in a shortened form in *The Winter's Tale* where, in characteristic fashion, clusters of associated images recur. Like Iago, Leontes remarks on the paddling palms and pinching fingers, and sets traps to ensnare the supposed lovers, telling us, "I am angling now" (I.ii.180). Othello in the midst of his torment asks,

> What sense had I in her stol'n hours of lust?
> I saw't not, thought it not; it harm'd not me.
> I slept the next night well, fed well, was free and merry;
> I found not Cassio's kisses on her lips.
> He that is robb'd, not wanting what is stol'n,
> Let him not know't, and he's not robb'd at all.
>
> (III.iii.338–43)[25]

Leontes likewise observes,

> There may be in the cup
> A spider steep'd, and one may drink; depart,
> And yet partake no venom (for his knowledge
> Is not infected), but if one present
> Th'abhorr'd ingredient to his eye, make known

24. "Whereas the singer thinks of his song in terms of a flexible plan of themes, some of which are essential and some of which are not, we think of it as a given text" Albert Lord, *The Singer of Tales*, p. 99.

25. All references are from *The Riverside Shakespeare,*, ed. G. Blakemore Evans (Boston, 1974).

How he hath drunk, he cracks his gorge, his sides,
With violent hefts.

                                                              (II.i.39–45)

Similarly we see Leontes, like Othello, remarking but more briefly, that
such "entertainment" as Hermione gives to Polixenes "May a free face put
on, derive a liberty / From heartiness, from bounty, fertile bosom, /
And well become the agent" (I.ii.111). "'Tis not to make me jealous,"
Othello remarks to Iago, "To say my wife is fair, feeds well, loves company, / Is free of speech, sings, plays, and dances [well];/Where virtue is,
these are more virtuous" (III.iii.184–186).

    The extent to which such lines reflect formulae which can be varied,
rather than an author simply repeating himself, is made even clearer by the
divers ways in which certain themes recur. Sometimes, as in the case of
Leontes and Othello, themes are attached to situations that are themselves
kinds of formulae. Thus we hear from Macbeth lines we have earlier heard
from Richard III. "I am in blood / Stepp'd in so far that, should I wade no
more," Macbeth says to Lady Macbeth, "Returning were as tedious as go
o'er" (III.iv.135–137). "But I am in / So far in blood," Richard III had
said, "that sin will pluck on sin. / Tear-falling pity dwells not in this eye"
IV.ii.63–65). And the lust which Richard tells Buckingham to attribute
to Edward in order to discredit him is later claimed by Malcolm when he
talks to Macduff. But the situations are not always so transparently allied.
We can understand why both Brutus and Othello remark on the means by
which what they see as sacrifice might be turned into murder. Brutus
makes the remark to Cassius when it is suggested that Mark Antony be
killed as well as Caesar. "Our course will seem too bloody," he says,
". . . Let's be sacrificers, but not butchers, Caius." Othello's remarks are
in response to Desdemona's profession of innocence before she is killed.

O perjur'd woman, thou dost stone my heart,
And [mak'st] me call what I intend to do
A murther, which I thought a sacrifice.

                                                              (V.ii.63–65)

The association is obviously with the manner of death, although differences in plot and differences in character make the line resonate in the two
plays in very different ways. And when Othello as well as Macbeth tells the

stars to hide their fire, we can see that the repetition comes less from a similarity of character than from a similarity of deed. The same reasoning seems to apply when both Antony and Claudio talk of meeting death as a bridegroom and when both Titus and Claudius remark on how concealed sorrow burns within.

More often, and more interesting because of what we learn about Shakespeare's uses of such a technique, formulae recur in unexpected places. In earlier plays an insufficient skill at what is basically a method of improvisation can give rise to lines that seem arbitrary and at times willful. Thus in speaking of Silvia to Valentine the Duke of Milan uses a formula that Shakespeare later made an integral part of the plot of *Lear*. Silvia is said to be peevish, sullen, forward, proud, disobedient, stubborn, lacking duty, and her pride has drawn his love from her.

> And where I thought the remnant of mine age
> Should have been cherish'd by her child-like duty,
> I now am full resolv'd to take a wife,
> And turn her out to who will take her in:
> Then let her beauty be her wedding-dow'r,
> For me and my possessions she esteems not.
>
> (III.i.74–79)

A similar instance can be seen in *King John*. Pandulph, speaking just after the marriage of Blanche to the Dolphin, is trying to persuade the King of France to ignore the marriage vow. His logic, at best, seems tortuous and one marvels at its success.

> For that which thou hast sworn to do amiss
> Is not amiss when it is truly done;
> And being not done, where doing tends to ill,
> The truth is then most done not doing it.
>
> (III.i.270–273)

From this observation Pandulph draws a conclusion.

> The better act of purposes mistook
> Is to mistake again; though indirect,
> Yet indirection thereby grows direct,
> And falsehood falsehood cures, as fire cools fire
>
> (III.i.274–277)

By the time of *Hamlet* Shakespeare had learned so well how to weave such
formulae into the fabric of his plays that Polonius's bait of falsehood to
take a carp of truth, his windlasses and assays of bias (II.i.59) look not only
backward toward the figure and the tale of the ghost, but forward to
Horatio's summary of the entire play. Asking Fortinbras to let him speak
to the "yet unknowing world / How these things came about," he says

> So shall you hear
> Of carnal, bloody, and unnatural acts,
> Of accidental judgments, casual slaughters,
> Of deaths put on by cunning and [forc'd] cause,
> And in this upshot, purposes mistook
> Fall'n on th' inventors' heads
>
> (V.ii.380–385)

In the mature playwright it is such skill in use that keeps a method
dependent upon repetition from creating plays that seem repetitious. The
same formula can be used to give us the illusion of distinct characters.
Brutus alone in his orchard when he reflects that "between the acting of a
dreadful thing/ And the first motion, all the interim is/Like a phantasma
or a hideous dream," (II.i.63) does not make us think of the Macbeth who
reflects that "present fears/Are less than horrible imaginings" (I.iii.137),
for the formula as Shakespeare rephrases it creates for the audience the
sense of terror in Macbeth's mind. And when Macbeth says, one assumes
to those on stage, just after the discovery of Duncan's body, those extraordinary lines,

> Had I but died an hour before this chance,
> I had liv'd a blessed time; for from this instant
> There's nothing serious in mortality.
>
> (II.iii.91–93)

we are unlikely to hear in them an echo of an earlier remark of Othello's,
simply because the context changes the sense of the formula being used.
Othello's remarks occur when he first greets Desdemona in Cypress.

> If it were now to die,
> 'Twere now to be most happy; for I fear
> My soul hath her content so absolute

That not another comfort like to this
Succeeds in unknown fate.

(II.i.189–193)

More telling in a way is the third variation of this formula. "Undone undone!" the old shepherd says to Perdita just after Polixenes has revealed himself. "If I might die within this hour, I have liv'd / To die when I desire" (IV.iv.460–462).

What we learn from such examples is that the formulaic method once associated with oral composition can create a more complexly rendered verbal structure than one might at first imagine, and the impression is only confirmed by even a brief glimpse at aural patterns within individual plays. Catherine Ing in discussing the structure of English airs shows what I think to be an essential aspect of aural patterning. In air poetry, she points out, the poet takes a phrase dictated by the needs of logic or emotion in its first use and treats "it as a model on which to mould another." Once the first line is established, we are given other lines of like length and structure to balance it as well as lines of simply related proportion to alternate with it. And she notes that in this kind of composition there are few limits to the varieties of phrase which can be recognized as having formal unity. [26]

We can trace a similar use of heard patterns in the opening of *Hamlet*. [27] Thus the play begins with Bernardo's "Who's there?," "What, is Horatio there?" and continues with Horatio's "What art thou that usurp'st this time of night?" and later in the play with Hamlet's "Is it the King?" and "Who is this they follow? And with such maimed rites?," "What is he whose grief Bears such an emphasis?" In a similar way Horatio's charge to the ghost, "Speak, speak, I charge thee speak," repeats Francisco's "Nay, answer me, Stand and unfold yourself," as Horatio's "But look, the morn in russet mantle clad / Walks o'er the dew of yon high eastward hill," repeats in its beginnings his earlier "But soft, behold! lo where it comes." These are essentially repetitions of forms of expression, syntactic in nature, varied within the play by context, but often, as Stephen Booth has

26. *Elizabethan Lyrics* (London, 1951), p. 135.
27. The discussion of *Hamlet* which follows I have used in a slightly different form in *Shakespeare and the Rhetoricians*.

shown,[28] attached to actions that are themselves forms of repetition. Thus at the re-entry of the ghost the same observers are seated in order to listen to a desired explanation; both action and phrase are repeated. "Well, sit we down," Horatio says before the first entry of the ghost. "Good now, sit down," Marcellus says prior to the second.

More interesting over the years to the critics in those studies of imagery of which Bentley complains have been the semantic repetitions in which a theme itself is repeated in varying ways. We see an instance of such varying in the enigmatic statement of Francisco's which Booth mentions as one example of the ways in which expectation in this scene is frustrated again and again. " 'Tis bitter cold, And I am sick at heart." If we see this remark not as one directed to a concern with character but rather initiated by a concern with pattern, it would seem to introduce a semantic thread that is varied first by Horatio's "This bodes some strange eruption to our state," and later with amplification by Hamlet's "O that this too too sallied flesh would melt, / Thaw, and resolve itself into a dew"—something we hear as we listen to the play. A particularly interesting example of this kind of varying occurs in Marcellus's question prior to the second appearance of the ghost, the question, as Booth points out, that wanted answering at the very beginning of the play—"Why this same strict and most observant watch / So nightly toils the subject of the land." It is yet another interrogative, and as such picks up and repeats a form first used in the opening lines of the play. It does answer the by now lapsed question about the reason for the watch. But appearing as it does at this particular point in the scene, immediately after Horatio's observation on the portent of the ghost, Marcellus's question both amplifies and varies the strange eruption to the state that Horatio foresees. It is one of the themes attached to the ghost. At the same time Marcellus's question makes possible a change in pace, so that Horatio, in developing yet another form of the theme with which the play opens, balances the staccato and even broken lines that mark the opening and the more recent appearance of the ghost with a leisurely narrative of enjambed lines in which not only the fight between two former kings but "the most high and palmy state of Rome /

28. "On the Value of Hamlet," *Literary Criticism: Idea and Act*, ed. W. K. Wimsatt (Berkeley, 1974), pp. 284–310.

A little ere the mightiest Julius fell" become part of the aural pattern of the play. An idea of ghosts is amplified and varied by means of a historical example. What the mind follows by means of the ear is a continuing elaboration of aural patterns that recur in varying shapes throughout the length of the play. Other critics have pointed out similar patterning in *Macbeth* in which both the first and second scenes begin, curiously enough, with questions, and in which the witches' "Fair is foul, and foul is fair," is echoed not only by Macbeth's use of the same words but by the sergeant's earlier "So from that spring whence comfort seem'd to come / Discomfort swells," and Banquo's "Why do you start, and seem to fear / Things that do sound so fair," even as the word *blood*, appearing in Duncan's opening words, is emphasized in the killing of Duncan and interlaced with that equivocation which defines the end.

Even when we look at plot as such a similar kind of repetition occurs. What we have learned of young Fortinbras from Horatio we learn again from Claudius. And the appearance of the ghost which we as audience have witnessed is described for us again by Horatio at the end of the next scene. And we see other kinds of repetition making possible other kinds of continuance—the death of Caesar, the death of Priam, the grief of Hecuba. This is the kind of structure that, following G. S. Kirk,[29] I have called cumulative. What we hear, as G. K. Hunter has pointed out, unlike what we read, is paratactic.[30] This does not mean that what we hear lacks any significant shape. Rather, the first scene of Hamlet, like the play in its entirety, articulates a significance which is determined as much by its repetitions as by its progressions. The remarks of Catherine Ing as well as the continuing work of Keith Brown[31] make me suspect that there is an order to such patterning that we are only beginning to understand. Yet it is possible even without an ear trained in the sixteenth century to hear patterns of recurrence as aural articulation of significance. We hear in the

29. See above n. 22.

30. "Shakespeare's Tragic Sense as It Strikes Us Today," *Shakespeare: Pattern of Excelling Nature*, ed. David Bevington and Jay L. Halio (Newark, 1978), pp. 81–87.

31. "'Form and Cause Conjoin'd': 'Hamlet' and Shakespeare's Workshop," *ShS*, XXVI (1973), 11–20.

cock and russet-mantled dawn a kind of closure which shapes the scene because we hear in it a variation of a pattern with which the scene began. [32]

IV

More than twenty-five years ago Raymond Williams in *Drama as Performance* showed the ways in which Shakespeare uses stage action in his plays as the occasion for much of his verse, and found in this oral device the technique that makes Shakespeare's acting text so different from Ibsen's. Shakespeare's verse tells the actors what to do. [33] That is because, like Gascoigne's, his dramatic verse is made out of the occasion of its saying, and so, like Gascoigne's, it is by Ricoeur's definition, even as printed, a form of speech. And insofar as such verbal structuring provides its own reference, the varying that grows out of the occasion is not only self-referring, as we said earlier of figures and of meter and rhyme, but referential to the occasion of its use. It refers "to that reality which can be pointed out 'around' the speaker, 'around,' so to speak, the instances of discourse itself." The instance of its discourse is the action of the play as it is played on the stage. Formal elaboration of occasion is in its origin and in its intent oral. Even a formal speaker speaks in terms of a given occasion, however fictive that occasion may be; his repetitions are verbal elaborations of that occasion, and they are meant for the ear.

Are they conceptual as well? This is essentially the question that Bentley's remarks raise, the question with which we began. "Even the most perceptive playgoer could never take in these verbal patterns by the ear alone," Bentley argues, "and the students of imagery do not maintain that he could." [34] But what about the students of performance? We have seen how the verbal means by which an occasion is elaborated are formulaic, and insofar as inscription is a kind of writing, it is not surprising that such "writing," when printed, can be significantly "read." We see an instance of such a reading by Cleanth Brooks in his discussion of a state-

32. G. S. Kirk calls this ring-composition, *Homer and the Oral Tradition*, p. 71. See J. B. Hainsworth, "The Criticism of an Oral Homer," *Journal of Hellenic Studies*, XC (1970), 97, Albert Lord, *Singer of Tales*, p. 92.

33. (London 1954, 1968; New York 1968).

34. "Shakespeare and the Readers of His Plays," p. 2.

ment Macbeth makes prior to the murder when he compares pity for Duncan to

> a naked new-born babe,
> Striding the blast, or heaven's cherubin, hors'd
> Upon the sightless couriers of the air
>
> (I.vii.21–23)

What Brooks does with these images is to trace their connections through the play, and so he looks at Macbeth's later description of the murdered Duncan in which the daggers are "unmannerly breech'd with gore," and at the explicit clothes imagery that Miss Spurgeon had discovered and at the many references to babes. He looks as well at what he sees as related images, those of growth and development, especially the imagery of plants. The number of such references, he remarks, can hardly be accidental, and for him finally the babe "signifies the future which Macbeth would control and cannot control." Thus "the logic of Macbeth's distraught mind . . . forces him to make war on children."[35] This seems a very questionable kind of reading today, and, in fact, it was attacked by Helen Gardner shortly after it appeared.[36] It grows out of the same kind of assumption that produced the seminal work of L. C. Knights and G. Wilson Knight. Shakespeare not only builds metaphors, but in so doing he creates a very rich context and he does so "with flexibility which must amaze the reader."[37]

Does the absence of the occasion, which is to say the absence of the temporal element, mean that such attempts in their method are wrong? When as early as *Romeo and Juliet* one hears an echo of "star-cross'd lovers" in Juliet's invocation of night in III.ii, in which she says of Romeo, "Come, night, come Romeo, come, thou, day in night, / For thou wilt lie upon the wings of night / Whiter than new snow upon a raven's back" and when one then hears her say, "Give me my Romeo, and, when I shall

35. "The Naked Babe and the Cloak of Manliness," *Approaches to Shakespeare*, ed. Norman Rabkin (New York, 1964), pp. 66–89. The quotations occur on p. 86. The essay originally appeared in *The Well Wrought Urn* (1947).

36. "A Reply to Cleanth Brooks," excerpted from a lecture given in 1953, in Rabkin, *Approaches to Shakespeare*, pp. 90–98.

37. Cleanth Brooks, "The Naked Babe," p. 89. See also pp. 75, 88.

die, / Take him and cut him out in little stars," it is difficult to imagine
that the patterning is *only* aural. Tybalt's discovery of Romeo at the
Capulet feast follows Romeo's "Forswear it, sight! / For I ne'er saw true
beauty till this night," even as his "this intrusion shall / Now seeming
sweet, convert to bitt'rest gall" precedes the lovers' exchange of vows.
Others have suggested how the ordering of the scene repeats in pattern the
exposition of the Prologue. It is the kind of variation both in pace and
mode that one might find in Mozart. In this instance the ideas being
suggested by means of dramatic order have been stated explicitly earlier.
In *Macbeth*, one suspects, the audience is assumed to be more sophisticated, or at least to have a more acute ear.

Obviously language patterns need not be conceptual. Yet the fact that
the trained ear expects and takes satisfaction in varied but imitated phrases
gave to both audience and dramatist a set of formal expectations. Hearing
Francisco say, "Who's there/" they waited to see how the phrase would be
woven through the play. And it is difficult to believe that what they heard
in listening for patterns did not help them to comprehend. Our only way
of knowing how they listened is to look at such evidence as we have.
Listening to Quince's prologue to Pyramus and Thisby, Theseus says,
"This fellow doth not stand upon points." Would an audience actually
have heard that the Prologue did not stand upon points, or did
Shakespeare put the words in Theseus's mouth to make sure that they did?
We have no way of knowing. But Puttenham at least suggests that the
best patterns in poetry are conceptual as well as aural. The auricular
figures, he says, reach only to the ear, the "sensable" "are made as well
tunable to the eare, as stirring to the minde," the rhetorical "may execute
both offices, and all at once to beautifie and geue sence and sententiousnes
to the whole language at large."[38] And Campion tells his readers that the
ear is a rational sense.[39] Beyond that the question is difficult to answer
according to the historical evidence, which is what Bentley rightly
demands.

But that is not quite the end of the matter. In a discussion of

38. *The Arte of English Poesie*, ed. Gladys Doidge Willcock and Alice Walker
(Cambridge, Eng., 1936), p. 196.

39. *Observations in the Art of English Poesie* (London, 1602), p. 5.

Shakespeare's style C. S. Lewis observes that "where Milton marches steadily forward, Shakespeare behaves rather like a swallow. He darts at the subject and glances away; and then he is back again before your eyes can follow him." The effect of this, Lewis argues, is that Shakespeare can use poetic language while creating at the same time a sense of realistic portrayal. Unable to utter without difficulty the precise, polished phrase that might encapsule the essence of their feelings, his characters appear true to life.[40] What such varying does, it seems to me, for all of Shakespeare's characters as they enact the play, is to create the illusion of improvisation, that illusion that Cicero wanted to create as well when he delivered his orations. That is in a sense the purpose of formulae. But that that impression is in some senses of the word an artistic illusion is proven by the uses of formulae themselves. The discussion of the formal means by which the drama is structured must obviously be different in its nature from the experience we have when we watch a play. G. Wilson Knight makes a similar kind of observation when he remarks that "there are throughout the play a set of correspondences which relate to each other independently of the time-sequence which is the story."[41] We have seen these correspondences before. They are oral, formal, and self-referring. G. Wilson Knight calls them spatial. I, following Derrida, see them as kinds of inscription, and I have argued that they formed a kind of writing, presented in oral form. Hence they do not constitute a script. What they create is a text written for oral performance. It is that text that G. Wilson Knight interprets, and it is that text that Shakespeare's actors played.

40. "Variation in Shakespeare and Others," *Selected Literary Essays* (Cambridge, Eng., 1969), pp. 74–87. The quotation appears on p. 75.

41. "On the Principles of Shakespeare Interpretation," *The Wheel of Fire* (London, 1930), p. 3.

"Soft, Who Have We Here?": The Dramatic Technique of The Old Wives Tale

JOAN C. MARX

I N RECENT YEARS critics have celebrated the folk narrative of *The Old Wives Tale*. In a country where many folktales of magic and "faierie" disappeared before nineteenth-century collectors could find them, Peele's play offers some of the earliest English evidence of these oral folk traditions,[1] and commentators have suggested that modern audiences "succumb to . . . [the play's] fairy-like atmosphere" and enjoy the "naïve" spell of old and powerful stories: of a young man compelled to assume a bear's form at night, of Golden Heads who rise from a well to reward two daughters, one selfish, the other kind; and of a hero who generously gives all he owns for a stranger's burial and is then guided by a magic helper.[2]

1. Katharine M. Briggs, Introduction to *A Dictionary of British Folk-Tales in the English Language* (Bloomington, Ind., 1971), I, A, 4.

2. A. K. McIlwraith, ed., *Five Elizabethan* Comedies (Oxford, 1934), p. xiii; and Frank Hook, ed., *The Old Wives Tale* by George Peele, in *The Life and Works of George Peele*, ed. Charles T. Prouty (New Haven, Conn., 1970), III, 365–366. See also Gwenan Jones, "The Intention of Peele's 'Old Wives' Tale,'" *Aberystwyth Studies*, VII (1925), 79–93; Thorleif Larsen, "'The Old Wives' Tale' by George Peele," *Transactions of the Royal Society of Canada*, Ser. 3, XXIX, sec. 2 (1935), 157–170; and M. C. Bradbrook, "Peele's *The Old Wives Tale*," *ES*, XLIII (1962), 323–330. The narratives incorporate the tale types of "The Kind and Unkind Girls" and "The Grateful Dead" and Motif D621.1.1, "Man by day, animal by night." Hook points out these folktale types and motifs (pp. 324–335) which have been classified by Antii Aarne and Stith Thompson in *The Types of the Folk-Tale*, 2d rev. ed. (Helsinki, 1961), and by Stith Thompson in *Motif-Index of Folk-Literature*, rev. ed. (Bloomington, Ind., 1955).

But one of the most remarkable qualities of this "pleasant, conceited Comedie," as its publisher called it, has been its ability to evoke another major and quite different critical view, one dominant in the first half of this century and still reappearing. In 1903 F. B. Gummere suggested that the play is "a saucy challenge of romance, where art turns, however timidly, upon itself."[3] The frame characters and mockery of Huanebango's boasts—his battles against "brasen gates, inchanted towers, . . . thunder and lightning"—make the play a remarkable predecessor to *The Knight of the Burning Pestle*: it is a gay spoof, a parody of romance.

I suggest that both of these perceptions, in some measure, are true. One group describes the play's genre as folktale and celebrates its enchantment, the audience's relaxation into "the cloudy fabric of a dream,"[4] the second sees the play as parody, focused on romance, and enjoys its sauciness and comic spirit. But each of these received critical views assumes that the play consists of only one genre. I propose instead that *The Old Wives Tale* is a comedy composed of several genres: folktale, romance, folk ritual, and farce.[5] Each of the genres appears in "straight," unparodied form,[6] and is juxtaposed with the others; no one of them rules the entire play. Instead, the play's extraordinary dramatic technique consists in slipping suddenly

3. F. B. Gummere, ed., *The Old Wives Tale* in *Representative English Comedies*, ed. C. M. Gayley (New York, 1903), I, 346. Others include: Felix Schelling, *Elizabethan Drama 1558–1642* (Boston, 1908), I, 136; G. P. Baker, "The Plays of the University Wits," *CHEL* (1910), V, 145–147; C. F. Tucker Brooke, *The Tudor Drama* (Boston, 1911), p. 242; Leonard R. N. Ashley, *George Peele* (New York, 1970), pp. 127 ff; John Doebler, "The Tone of George Peele's *The Old Wives Tale*," *ES*, LIII (1972), 412–421.

4. Janet Spens's image of a dream for *The Old Wives Tale* appears in *Elizabethan Drama* (London, 1922), pp. 53–54, and recurs in David H. Horne, Introduction to *The Life and Works of George Peele*, ed. Prouty, I, 90, and Bradbrook, p. 329.

5. It is one form of "threshold work," to use the terms of Gary Saul Morson, one where "mutually exclusive sets of conventions govern a work," and where "generic incompatibility" is created by "embedding or juxtaposing sections of radically heterogeneous material. The generic conventions governing individual sections may be clear, but the laws of their combination are not." "Threshold Art," in *The Boundaries of Genre: Doestoevsky's Diary of a Writer and the Traditions of Literary Utopia* (Austin, Tex., Forthcoming, 1981).

6. Huanebango's parody is an exception which will be discussed.

from one genre to another.[7] Such unexpected shifts create a mixture of surprise and daring—a comic sauciness—closely resembling, though differing from, the effect of parody.

If we consider the song of the Golden Head, for example, its chant creates the conventional spell of folktale. The magic head which rises from a well is a folk motif, part of a folktale type, "The Heads in the Well,"[8] and the song evokes folktale's style and mood:

> Gently dip, but not too deepe,
> For feare you make the golden beard to weepe,
> Faire maiden white and red,
> Stroke me smoothe, and combe my head,
> And thou shalt have some cockell bread.[9]

The chant addresses the maiden with the familiar "white and red," and the song's short rhythms, full and half rhymes, recur in the lulling insistence of a magic charm.[10] Wooing and demanding in the same moment, the Head asks for certain gestures from the girl—"stroke me smoothe," "dip, but not too deepe"—for the virile, literally disembodied, golden beard. Like the demands of the frog who must be taken up and placed by the girl's plate or laid on her pillow, these requests are imbued with a powerful yet unacknowledged sexuality, one that often marks the gestures required of maidens by the animals and monsters of folktale.[11]

The same kind of straight, unparodied rendering of generic convention appears at the moment the "wandring knight," Eumenides, rescues the princess and sues for her hand. Yet the genre embodied is not folktale but romance.

---

7. I will stress the "tale," but its generic shifts are prepared for by the mild stylistic shifts of the Induction, from "*O coelum! O terra! O maria!*" to "Hearke this is Ball my dogge," from "Cupid hath led our yong master to the faire Lady and she is the only Saint that he hath sworne to serve" to "wee commit him to his wench."

8. "The Heads in the Well" is a subtype of "The Kind and Unkind Girls"; see Warren E. Roberts, *The Tale of the Kind and the Unkind Girls* (Berlin, 1958).

9. *The Old Wives Tale*, ed. Frank Hook; all following references will be to this edition.

10. This recalls Madge's "white as snowe, and as redd as bloud," Motif Z65.1.

11. Bruno Bettelheim suggests this sexuality in Grimm's "The Frog-King" and other fairytales, in *The Uses of Enchantment* (New York, 1976), pp. 277 ff.

Thou fairest flower of these westerne parts:
Whose beautie so reflecteth in my sight,
As doth a Christall mirror in the sonne:
For thy sweet sake I have crost the frosen Rhine,
Leaving faire Po, I saild up Danuby . . . [12]

(ll. 850–854)

The knight can express the maiden's beauty in a self-conscious rhetoric of "Christall mirror" and "fairest flower," and her "sweet" self focuses his vision and quest. [13] His stance is individual and heroic, and he sails a far-ranging, exotic, and yet a known world, one of "Po" and "Danuby." [14] He is not a careful walker in the fields of folk magic, bending to the rhythmic instructions of old men and singing Heads, traveling in a dark, unmapped territory to find a well of the "water of life."

But each such conventional moment in the play is continually being cut short; one mood, one range of style suddenly changes to another. The pleasure at abruptly arriving in new territory is akin to the comic liberation described by Freud; it is a burst of unexpected freedom, a sudden release from the expected tones and gestures—the conventional restraints—of a genre.

The change in mood may be as great and the translation of terms as neat as Zantippa's response to the Golden Head. In the folktale action of "the Kind and Unkind Girls" the shrewish daughter, seeking a husband, approaches the magic well with her pitcher; as she nears, the Golden Head rises and chants, "Stroke me smoothe, and combe my head, / And thou shalt have some cockell bread." [15] Zantippa draws back, cries, "Cockell callest thou it boy, faith ile give you cockell bread," and delivers the Head a blow with the pitcher. Both the rude "boy" and rough blow go much

12. The last two lines as well as ll. 855–856 are imitated from Robert Greene's *Orlando Furioso* (Hook, pp. 307, 442).

13. Eugène Vinaver describes the rise of a portrayal of "feeling" in medieval romance, *The Rise of Romance* (Oxford, 1971), p. 26; Erich Auerbach explores the knight's concentration of his quest on "feats of arms, and love" in *Mimesis* (Princeton, N.J., 1953), p. 140.

14. R. W. Southern discusses the knight's individual stance in *Making of the Middle Ages*, p. 244, cited by Vinaver, p. 2; this is the landscape of Italian rather than medieval romance, as the latter is described by Auerbach, pp. 128–129.

15. Roberts describes the conventional action, p. 119.

beyond the sister's conventional unkindness; in addition Zantippa is promising a comic transformation of the love charm of the Golden Head, its offered "cockell bread." These loaves had a crust which rose in sexually suggestive swells; Zantippa's "cockell bread" will be the bumps she can raise on the enchanted Head. [16] Funny, crude, and disrespectful, her action breaks the spell of folk magic. But folktale and folk magic are no more travestied by their disappearance and the sudden advent of farce than romance is satirized at the moment Sacrapant calls his spirits. Having shown himself a romance enchanter by falling in love with and courting a beautiful woman, idealizing her power in Renaissance terms ("See where she coms from whence my sorrows grow"), [17] Sacrapant offers his captive mistress whatever she desires. But when he turns to fulfill her request, his summons is a folktale charm.

> Spred table spred;
> Meat, drinke and bred

16. It seems clear from the context that "cockell bread" had some associations with marriage, love, or sexuality, but its range of associations during the Renaissance is not known. We can assume that it looked like the *pain coquillé* of the French, with swellings in the crust, described by Paul Robert, "coquiller," in *Dictionnaire alphabétique et analogique*, 6 vols. (Paris, 1951). Aubrey's comment of 1697, usually cited to explain the bread, describes young maids drawing up their skirts and rocking back and forth, singing of the "moulding of Cockle-bread." He also refers to an early medieval text describing bread used as a love charm and made while a woman exposed her naked buttocks; see William J. Thoms. ed., *Anecdotes and Traditions* (London, 1839), pp. 94–95. The association of buttocks with the bread is easy to make, but it is not evident that "moulding cockle-bread" is the bread's only or major association. During the fifteenth century such bread was being sold by French bakers and regulated in price; in the sixteenth, "coquillé" is used to describe an attractive stomach; see Emile Littré, "coquiller," in *Dictionnaire de la langue française*, 7 vols. (Paris, 1956). Cake and bread, including *gateaux phalliques*, were still being used symbolically during courtship in France, in recent years; see Arnold van Gennep, *Manuel de Folklore français Contemporain* (Paris, 1946), vol. I, pt. 1, pp. 265, 275. I would tentatively suggest that the reference is not obscene. Cockell bread is again included in the Head's second song, again an incantation, but this time it occurs within, rather than at the end of the chant; a lewd reference here would break the spell very awkwardly.

17. Folktale's enchanters may, however, have an implicit sexual bond with their princesses, as in "Beauty of the World," in *West Irish Folk-Tales and Romances*, ed. and trans. William Larminie (London, 1893), pp. 155–167.

> Ever may I have,
> What I ever crave:
> When I am spred,
> For meate for my black cock,
> And meate for my red.
>
> (ll. 367–73)

This is no vision of heaven or demons, but a spell with country roosters, the same call for a small feast in the fields that appears in Grimm's folktale of "The Wishing-Table, the Gold-Ass, and the Cudgel in the Sack." [18]

Like parody, this technique creates a gay mood and an awareness of form. But if the familiar image of parody is that of a distorted mirror, offering an exaggerated view of something outside the work itself—the true, substantial figure—then this play is more like several clowns gesturing at each other. [19] Each bit has its own life and substance, and the true is followed by "something else" rather than an insubstantial reflection of itself. What was there goes back in the well and is replaced by the new; the switch may cause a sense of loss, but the major sensation it produces is a mixture of surprise and daring, a sense of "Soft, who have we here?" to be asked by the audience as well as the Pages. [20]

Herbert Goldstone has been one critic to resist classifying the play as either naïve folktale or romance parody; yet for him these shifts serve such unlikely ends as rendering the characters more humane and highly artificial genres, such as folktale, more believable. [21] Instead the play has the slip and whirl of a fast carnival ride or the funny and graceful ice skating of the vaudeville comic, Ben Blue; an audience poised on the tip of romance, "Berecynthia, let us in . . . / And heare the Nightingale," suddenly whips into the sturdy "Now for a husband, house and home" (ll. 609–611).

---

18. Sylvia Lyons-Render cites the motif, the "magic table supplies food and drink" (D1472.1.7), in "Folk Motifs in George Peele's *The Old Wives Tale*, *TFSB*, XXVI (1960), 62–71.

19. See, for example, "Burlesque and parody," in M. H. Abrams's *A Glossary of Literary Terms* (New York, 1957).

20. Ll. 140, 533, 539, Madge's variant (l. 129), and Sacrapant's question (l. 393).

21. Herbert Goldstone, "Interplay in Peele's *The Old Wives Tale*," *Boston Univ. Studies in English*, IV (1960), 205 ff.

These effects may feel more "real"; critics from Gummere onward have talked about "realism in diction" and its undercutting of romance.[22] Yet the change may be to a homelier but equally artificial style. When the Two Brothers enter, the formal rhetoric of their lament heightens their apostrophe to the power of fortune above, "O fortune cruell, cruell and unkind, / Unkind in that we cannot find our sister," and when Erestus appears, his short, heavy rhythms and earthbound concerns, "Hips and Hawes, and stickes and strawes, and thinges that I gather on the ground my sonne," create a small tumble from romance to folktale, one made more humorous by the Brothers' new attention to food, "Hips and Hawes, and stickes and strawes, why is that all your foode father?" But the new style is equally patterned, equally artificial.

The shift will also consist in a change of attitude as much as verbal style. When Huanebango courts Zantippa at the well of the water of life, theirs is a courtship molded by folktale justice; the beautiful "unkind" shrew has been awarded the deaf man who can appreciate her beauty but not her tongue. Yet her acceptance suddenly glimpses both a cynicism and a mutability foreign to folktale. She shrugs, "Lobb be your comfort, and Cuckold bee your destenie: Heare you sir; and if you will have us, you had best say so betime." The change in diction is less marked than the new attitude; instead of the folktale finality "they lived together in peace and contentment" or "they quarrelled for the rest of their lives," her resignation to a fool and "Cuckold" envisions compromise and an unsettled life, a future with other men.

To register the necessary surprise at such changes, Peele's audience would have needed a knowledge of the play's genres and boundaries, an awareness they would in fact have possessed even as they jostled into seats or standing room.[23] For such an awareness of each of the play's generic groups would have been awakened by a wide variety of experiences. The play does not depend on an acquaintance with one specific work in a given genre, on Greene's *Orlando Furioso* or "The Wal at the Warld's End," but

22. Gummere, p. 341.
23. An audience, like Guillén's writer beginning to compose, would have *a priori* notions of genre; see Claudio Guillén, *Literature as System* (Princeton, N.J., 1971), pp. 125–128.

merely on an exposure to some members of each general group: to *Olyver of Castylle* or *Guy of Warwick*, to their own village's Plough Monday or a mother's report of it, to the clown's jigs at The Theatre or *A Hundred Merry Tales*, to "The Robber Bridegroom" or "Snow-White and Rose-Red," told by an uncle or nurse. [24] Such experience of the members of a generic group would in turn create an awareness of the group's characteristics and its boundary, that limit which demarcates its characteristics and excludes others. [25] (This does not mean that there is a prescribed list of characteristics which marks every member of a generic group, for characteristics are shared in a partial way. Among three folktales, for example, the first and second might share talking animals, the second and third, a stepdaughter's quest. But even with such sharing, there is a family grouping of characteristics and a boundary to the group.)[26] My imagined Elizabethan in Peele's audience could expect certain gestures and styles of a particular genre and know that others are excluded: introspection is not part of folktale.

Tilting the play, readying it for shifts across these generic boundaries, are the small surprises within the genres. Conventional, expected gestures are frequently skewed, and create in turn a constant precariousness. There may be too many motifs—Erestus is transformed to an old-man *and* a bear; or a sequence of motifs is reversed—Celanta finds her husband before she encounters the magic donor, the Golden Head; or what is simply "not done" is done—Erestus thanks Lampriscus for his quite apropos gift, "Thankes neighbor, . . . Honny is alwaies welcome to the Beare," and in

24. Briggs gives two English analogies to Peele's "Kind and Unkind Girls": "The Wal at the Warld's End" and "Three Gold Heads." *Olyver of Castylle* was published in English in 1518 and known in 1575; see *"The Hystorye of Olyver of Castylle,"* ed. Gail Orgelfinger, (Ph.D. dissertation, University of Chicago, 1978), pp. 83, 108. (I have modernized the "v".) Charles Baskervill describes the farce plots of the jigs, used as afterpieces and found in the jestbooks, in *The Elizabethan Jig* (Chicago, 1929), pp. 95, 233, and *passim*. "The Robber Bridegroom" is referred to in *Much Ado about Nothing*, I.i.216; "Snow-White and Rose-Red" seems to lie behind this play (Briggs, I, A, 4).

25. E. D. Hirsch describes the generic group as one form of "type," in *Validity in Interpretation* (New Haven, Conn., 1967); for "type," see pp. 64 and Appendix III.A, for "genre," see pp. 71 ff., 114–115.

26. As Robert C. Elliott points out in "The Definition of Satire," the boundary is a *"decision"* rather than a *"factual"* question (quoted by Guillén, pp. 130–131).

that second seems to bring his nighttime transformation into daylight, to casually acknowledge a dark, binding enchantment as an alternative image of himself.[27]

The most colorful and striking examples of such shifts within scenes may well be the Huanebango scenes: his two encounters of Erestus and Sacrapant and his courtship of Zantippa at the well. Their vividness is due partly to Huanebango's exaggeration as a figure of romance, partly to the triple variety of genres—romance, farce, and folktale—rapidly exchanged.

The mighty Juan y Bango is an apparent exception to the general notion that the play's technique lies in generic shifts rather than parody.[28] With his soaring, hollow boasts, his combat with "thunder and lightning" and search for peerless "Beautie," he clearly undercuts the assumptions of romance, its individual heroism and quests, and parodies the genre. Yet as a comic braggart, Huanebango is only weakly parodic. If *he* frames the objections to romance's assumptions, then romance, rather than being laughed at, is reasserted.[29] Analogously, when the braggart soldier, Sir Tophas, worships his hag in Lyly's *Endimion*, he deflects ridicule from the hero's adoration of Cynthia. In the end, even as a figure of parody, Huanebango serves the play's generic shifts: essentially he functions as a figure of romance, his parody making him only a more extravagant, colorful representative.[30] Eumenides, for example, could replace Huanebango at the well. Zantippa's replies would seem cruder, her suitor less comic and more vulnerable, but the basic scheme would remain: a romance knight courting "peerelesse" Beauty would still kneel before a folktale girl seeking "husband, house and home." But since Huanebango is exaggerated, he makes the distance between genres, e.g., between

27. Most folktale animals cannot mention their enchantments; see, for example, Grimm's "The Frog Prince" and "The Golden Bird." Sarah Clapp notes a number of such changes in "Peele's Use of Folk-Lore in *The Old Wives' Tale*," *Univ. of Texas Studies in English*, VI (1926), pp. 146–156.

28. Bradbrook gives his name its Spanish form, p. 328.

29. William Empson points out that a play of "heroic swashbucklers" will include "a comic cowardly swashbuckler" in order to keep the audience from mocking the heroes, *Some Versions of Pastoral* (Norfolk, Conn., n.d.), p. 30.

30. As John Felstiner says, "because all art entails some exaggeration of neutral fact, caricature and parody exemplify the larger genres they fall within," *The Lies of Art* (New York, 1972), p. 136.

romance and folktale—the territory sped over, as it were—greater and more apparent, more vivid and comic. He also helps romance accommodate farce. For the two genres sit oddly together; the cynicism, coarseness, and hunger for physical things in farce are often romance's direct enemies.[31] But as a comic extreme of romance, Huanebango can tolerate farce's vulgarity and shoves. Erestus's aside about Huan's mistress, "Faire inough, and farre inough from thy fingering sonne," is crude as it is, but its humor when addressed to the grand Huanebango, lauding an "earthly Goddesse," would be lost if directed at Eumenides.

The most remarkable achievement of these scenes is their coherence. Even with swift, broad shifts, from the exaggeration of romance on the one hand to farce on the other, there is no muddle; the genres remain clear, the slips evident. The quick switches in Booby's roles form one of the most striking instances. When Huanebango first enters with Booby, for example, the knight is manifestly a braggart soldier, accompanied like Lyly's Sir Tophas by a companion and subordinate. Like Epiton, Sir Tophas's page, Booby furnishes his knight with "straight lines" which make him reveal his foolishness.

BOOBY

Doo you heare sir; had not you a Cosen, that was called Gustecerydis?

HUANEBANGO

Indeede I had a Cosen, that somtime followed the Court infortunately, and his name Bustegustecerydis.

BOOBY

O Lord I know him well: hee is the knight of the neates feete.

---

31. Anthony Caputi suggests that among the essential qualities of "vulgar comedy" are its emphasis on physicality and its coarseness (both a "coarseness of grain in the image" presented and a "relatively simple and uncomplicated" response from the beholder), in *Buffo* (Detroit, 1978), pp. 175–185. An example of the strikingly different viewpoints of romance and farce toward the same action is the dwarf's awakening of a household as a young knight leaves a girl's bedroom in *Amadis of Gaul*. This is the stuff of farce, but the dwarf is seen as contemptible; trans. Edwin B. Place and Herbert C. Behn (Lexington, Ky., 1974), Book I, chap. 12, pp. 132–135. The conflict of the two when juxtaposed is illustrated by Delia's magic wishes (e.g., for "the veriest knave in all Spaine"); set against romance they seem low and unworthy of her. This is one shift in the play which fails.

HUANEBANGO
O he lov'd no Capon better, he hath oftentimes deceived his boy
of his dinner, that was his fault, good Bustegusteccerydis.

(ll. 291–296)

Yet the moment before, Booby appeared not as a petite Epiton, a younger, cleverer version of Sir Tophas, one who shares his knight's assumptions that great deeds, love, wit, and rhetoric are important, but as a simple, coarse "countriman," leagues away from Huanebango's aspirations, someone who, when he heard of adventures with "thunder and lightning" and the search for "Beautie," replied, "Nowe sir if it bee no more but running through a little lightning and thunder, and riddle me riddle me whats this, Ile have the wench from the Conjurer if he were ten Conjurers." At one minute, in Epiton's style, Booby is parrying false Latin with the knight; in the next he is complaining—simple, good-natured lout that he is—that he cannot understand phrases like "foyson of the earth." (With hindsight Booby may be said to shift between Moth and Dull of *Love's Labor's Lost.*) In addition to these shifts, by the end of the scene Erestus has asked the knight to share his food, a conventional folktale test.[32] Huan fails, and in his place, Booby, the generous country lad, wins. In the next second, the new folktale hero calls good-bye, quits Erestus and his novel role, and runs to catch his commander, the grandiloquent Huanebango. The shifts are dizzying yet clear.

M. C. Bradbrook has suggested that *The Old Wives Tale* should be considered a "medley play," one whose structure consists only in cramming in as many "brief sequences, with as much scenic variety and multiplication of characters" as possible.[33] But what distinguishes Peele's play from her two examples, the *Rare Triumphs of Love and Fortune* and *The Cobler's Prophecy*, and serves to argue the artful, rather than hotchpotch, nature of *The Old Wives Tale*, is the fact that the other plays make no attempt to contrast different styles or highlight strange meetings. *Love and Fortune* does not display the same variety of characters as *The Old Wives Tale*, but *The Cobler's Prophecy* does; it includes such characters in its cast

---

32. Food must be given everyone on journey, Motif C675.
33. Bradbrook, p. 326.

as: Mercury, Gray Friar, Folly, Cobler's Wife, and Charon. [34] Yet these
characters move in a gray, common air. Almost anyone could come onstage, and almost anyone does, but the meeting of the Souldier and the
Muses, for example, is marked only by the momentary, coy surprise of the
Muses: "O sisters shift we are betraid, / Another man I see" (ll. 481–
482). There is none of the vivid, colorful incongruity of Huanebango, heir
to Polimackeroeplacydus, swirling his Latin around a folktale girl at the
well of the water of life, while she replies, "Foe, what greasie groome have
wee here?" [35]

However, such frequent, multiple incongruities require some continui-
ties in order not to fragment the play into a collection of bits. To this end,
besides the weaving of plots, there are recurring phrases and rhythms. [36]
"Frollicke franion" and "Aprill of my age" fall from different lips, and as
Frank Hook has remarked, even when long lines like "Fortune cruell,
cruell and unkind" change to the quick "Hips and Hawes, and stickes and
strawes," or when verse changes to prose, from "Hips and Hawes" to "I
will give thee as good a Gowne of gray as ever thou diddest weare," the
strong effects of meter and patterning continue. [37] Clunch, bewildered by

---

34. In *Love and Fortune* the characters range from courtiers to a hermit and his servant to
the gods; plot lines are few and basically clear, and the worlds of gods and men are clearly
separated; *The Rare Triumphs of Love and Fortune*, in *A Select Collection of Old English Plays*,
ed. W. Carew Hazlitt (London, 1874), vol. VI. Robert Wilson, *The Cobler's Prophecy*, ed.
A. C. Wood (n.p., 1914); I have modernized the long *s*.

35. How extraordinary this combination is may be suggested in part by other braggarts:
Don Armado exercises himself and his Latin in a court transplanted to the country but not a
landscape with a magic well, and Sir Brian le Foy of the early romance, *Clyomon and
Clamydes*, though allied with a magic dragon, never appears with the dragon or any other
supernatural apparatus.

36. Hook points out that the "essential" threads of the narratives are neatly woven and
sustained, p. 343. But the omission of Huanebango's release from enchantment has been
claimed as evidence of textual abridgment; see, for example, Harold Jenkins, "Peele's Old
Wives Tale," *MLR*, XXXIV (1939), 177–185, and Bradbrook, p. 325. Even Hook
suggests that seeing Huanebango released would be "dramatically satisfying." Yet this is a
misunderstanding of the folktale of the play. It would not be satisfying to annul the
marriages, find the two daughters once more without husbands, and the folktale achievement of evenhanded justice an illusion. It would be worse to preserve the marriages and
witness the respective pain and disappointment.

37. Hook, pp. 361–364.

others' references to Vulcan and hobgoblins, still manages a graceful, unsmithlike, "What make you in my territories at this time of the night?" and the rowdy Wiggen threatens the Churchwarden with both pikestaff and Latin. There is a certain Lylian harmony to the language although it is never toned to Lyly's single, silver pitch.

The frame characters (the Pages and Madge) provide another major continuity during the Tale, for they serve as a kind of neutral ground for characters and styles. Unlike other frame characters—the Grocer and his Wife in *The Knight of the Burning Pestle* or the courtiers who watch "Pyramus and Thisbe" in *Midsummer Night's Dream*, for instance—they question and explain at breaks in the action, rather than interrupting it, and their comments serve first to voice the theater audience's surprise, its concurrent reaction of "Soft, who have we here?" and then to accept—and in that way draw together—the play's discrete sequences, e.g., Erestus and Lampriscus discussing dowries and the singing Harvesters.

The play also limits its generic contrasts. Rather than being an open-ended series of styles,[38] the play slips among the closely related genres of romance, folktale, folk ritual, and farce. Although each of these genres has its own boundary, they share characteristics so that their tangent, common boundaries are "thick"; folktale will share a man in bear's shape with romance, and folk ritual, like folktale, will manifest a Golden Head.[39] (Romance and farce, as I have suggested, are quite disparate, but each of these genres is closely related to the other two.) Such sharing of motifs and attitudes offers a coherence to *The Old Wives Tale*, even as it shifts, which would be missing from a play with slips among more unlike genres, e.g., pastoral, satire, and tragedy.[40]

---

38. Goldstone describes such an open-ended series.

39. Hirsch discusses thick boundaries, p. 45. "Snow-White and Rose-Red" has a prince as bear, and Bradbrook notes William of Palerne's similar enchantment, p. 325n. Brand reports a "Harvest Queen" with ears of corn in *Brand's Popular Antiquities of Great Britian*, ed. W. Carew Hazlitt (London, 1905), p. 308. Farce, which owes much of its origins to folk ritual (see Caputi, pp. 40–94), shares with it themes and styles, e.g., the revolt of the young against old and sexual ribaldry.

40. Eugene M. Waith discusses the conflict of attitudes which arises from a combination of pastoral and satire in *The Pattern of Tragicomedy in Beaumont and Fletcher* (New Haven, Conn., 1952), pp. 71 ff.

But an emphasis on the thick boundaries of the play's genres brings us close to where we began: the critical views of the play which have blurred those boundaries by perceiving the play as one rather than several distinct genres. The major, obvious result of losing this distinction of genres has been the loss of the play's incongruities and shifts. Less evident and lost with them, as a further and ironic consequence, has been the fresh awareness of different genres—their discrete or shared attitudes and values—which such incongruities afford. [41]

Folk ritual, for example, manifest largely in the Harvester scenes, has been barely noted. [42] Instead this genre's moments have been thought "extraneous" to the play's structure; they offered incidental opportunities for "costly display" of costumes or "rustic atmosphere." [43] The anonymous figures of the Harvesters appear early in the Tale, first, after the beggar, Lampriscus, has consulted with Erestus about his daughters, and then again after Wiggen's rowdy chase of the Churchwarden. They interact with no other characters of the Tale and have no part in any of the plots. Each time they appear singing; the second time, when they come in "with women in their hands," they may dance as well. [44]

> All yee that lovely lovers be, pray you for me,
> Loe here we come asowing, asowing,
> And sowe sweete fruites of love:
> In your sweete hearts well may it prove.
>
> (ll. 250–253)

> Loe heere we come areaping, areaping,
> To reape our harvest fruite,
> And thus we passe the yeare so long,
> And never be we mute.
>
> (ll. 535–538)

41. An essential point of the Russian Formalists, e.g., Shklovsky, was: "whenever a text can be firmly classed as anomalous, the outlines of the class or classes that exclude it are themselves sharpened . . . a good way to illustrate a rule is to violate it strategically and ostentatiously. Transgressions *mark* boundaries," Morson, "Threshold Art."

42. Bradbrook notes the "rural seasonal games" of the Harvesters, p. 326.

43. Doebler, p. 418; Hook, p. 372; Larsen, p. 168.

44. Hook, p. 337. Such figures on a stage, with several women instead of folk ritual's one or two, would probably be associated with the masques as well; Hook suggests the likeness.

The songs address the audience more directly than the speeches of other characters,[45] and their immediacy is emphasized by the punning bisexuality of the first lyric: "your sweete heartes" courts the women in the audience and enlists the men as allies. Since each of these songs consists of a single stanza repeated (as the stage directions point out), they have a mild incantatory effect, and their metaphor of sowing and reaping—which portrays men's search for women—envisions human sexuality as part of nature's fertility.[46]

Such folk figures, once as familiar in English life as Father Nicholas is today, and though still surviving in such rare groups as the Marshfield Paper Boys,[47] have almost completely disappeared. The "guizers" or "plough jacks" would appear in their own villages in processions and stationary ceremonies.[48] They might be clothed in "normal" or working dress or in the more extraordinary folk costume of the Marshfield players, their bodies covered with shreds of paper until they resemble vaguely conical, haystack-shaped masses.[49] Contemporary Elizabethan references allow glimpses of them: Spenser describes June as a procession of "players" carrying plough irons and dressed in "leaves," the originals of the Marshfield paper shreds;[50] Nashe's Harvest, referred to as a "Plough-Swain," is dressed in "thatch," and his Reapers, calling a traditional harvest cry, demand the conventional quête of offering.[51] Such plough jacks, chanting and moving in a familiar ritual, would be both members of

---

45. There are brief one-line addresses to the audience, but none is sustained.

46. Goldstone suggests that the Harvesters create "a parallel between reaping and sowing in the cycle of seasons and in love, both of which are parts of nature," p. 212.

47. The Marshfield players are pictured in Alan Brody's *The English Mummers and Their Plays* (Philadelphia, 1970), pp. 33 ff.

48. *Ibid.*, p. 4, and *passim*.

49. T. F. Ordish describes ploughmen "in clean smock-frocks" as well as "reapers with sickles" in a Plough Monday procession (quoted by Hook, p. 427).

50. Michael J. Preston, "The Folk Play: An Influence on the *Faerie Queene*," *AN&Q*, VIII (1969), 38–39. Margaret Dean-Smith discusses the relationship of leaves and paper in "Folk-Play Origins of the English Masque," *Folk-Lore*, LV, (1954), 74–86.

51. R. B. McKerrow notes their folk-ritual cry in his edition of Thomas Nashe's *Summer's Last Will and Testament*, in *The Works of Thomas Nashe* (Oxford, 1958), vol. III. Bradbrook points out a general resemblance of Peele's figures to Nashe's, p. 327. Brody discusses the quête as a ritual practice, p. 14 n.

the community and removed from it, special luck-bringers set apart by ritual action. [52]

In *The Old Wives Tale* this anonymous group of chanting men, who sing of fertility and confront the audience directly, offer some of the boldest discontinuities of the play. Each time they appear, their lyricism directly follows a scene of folktale which has flashed into the cynical or raucous tone of farce (Lampriscus's thankfulness that his two wives are dead, Wiggen's threats to the "whorson scald Sexton"), and each time their melodic songs precede a Huanebango-and-Booby scene which shifts between parodied romance, folktale, and farce. With their first appearance, the Harvesters can make it clear that the shifts which have constantly been occurring, but in milder forms, are the deliberate, major technique of the play.

Yet the Harvesters also share two important attitudes with romance and folktale, respectively: a celebration of lovers and an awareness of a supernatural presence in nature. Their shaping of these attitudes, their particular vision, is peculiar to themselves—a point we will return to—but the Harvesters' songs reinforce the positive, ideal, and supernatural in the other genres and, in so doing, help to preserve the distinct presences of folktale and romance in the play. This is particularly true in the first scenes, when the range of the play is being established and when, at the same time, folktale is frequently replaced by farce and romance usually appears as parody. Without some reassertion, the celebration of lovers and the acknowledgment of the supernatural might well be corroded and dissolved by the cynical and everyday. To take a specific instance: if Erestus and Lampriscus were immediately followed by Huanebango and Booby, without the Harvesters' first song, it is likely that future moments of lyricism and enchantment—Sacrapant's admiration of Delia or the chant of the Golden Head—would be heard as parody. As it is, the Harvesters are essential in maintaining the play's wide range in tone and attitude and the consequent distinction of its genres.

Unlike folk ritual, folktale and romance have been perceived, but they have then been obscured in a different way. They have been blended together either by describing the two genres as one, as in "an old-fashioned

52. Brody, pp. 16, 21, 28.

romantic tale, a fairy story,"[53] or, in a more Procrustean style, by relegating all motifs to one genre or the other, e.g., "all that Peele has borrowed from romantic sources are the names of some of his persons."[54] The two have such a thick boundary that romance not only owes many of its individual motifs to folktale, but an entire tale type like the Grateful Dead, which appears in *The Old Wives Tale*, can occur both in romance—in *Olyver of Castylle* and *Sir Amadace*—and in folktale—in "Beauty of the World," "Jack the Master," and "The King of Ireland's Son."[55] It is possible as a result to have a moment which could belong to either genre, e.g., Eumenides' speech, "This man hath left me in a Laborinth" (ll. 449 ff.), after his encounter with Erestus. Here Eumenides, bewildered by Erestus's mysterious instructions, could be either a folklore hero or a knight on a quest; it would be unprofitable to apportion such a moment to one genre or the other. Nevertheless, even with their thick boundary, the two genres are distinct: most scenes or moments, even of a tale type common to both genres, are visibly rendered in one or the other genre, are characterized by one or the other's attitude and style. Perceiving these differences in generic moments, in their attitudes and styles, will allow in turn an awareness of the genres' differing values.

G. H. Gerould has abstracted the conventional action of the Grateful Dead:

A man finds a corpse lying unburied, and out of pure philanthropy procures interment for it at great personal inconvenience. Later he is met by the ghost of the dead man, who in many cases promises him help on condition of receiving, in return, half of whatever he gets. The hero obtains a wife (or some other reward), and, when called upon, is ready to fulfil his bargain as to sharing his possessions.

(p. x)

Two of these "grateful dead" scenes in *The Old Wives Tale*, the discovery of the body and the magic helper's first reward of the hero, can be identified as folktale rather than romance. The scene in which Wiggen and Corebus quarrel with church officials, who claim that burial fees are needed to roof

53. McIlwraith, p. xii. Doebler speaks of "fairy-tale chivalric romance," p. 418.

54. Larsen, p. 161; see also Hook, p. 360.

55. G. H. Gerould, *The Grateful Dead*, Pub. 60 of the Folk-Lore Society (London, 1908), pp. 7–25.

a church, is marked by an everyday practicality. This same quality characterizes the simple discovery of the body in "The King of Ireland's Son," where a knight sees a funeral procession coming down the road and a man puts "a writ down on the corpse for five pounds," and that in "Jack the Master," where Jack stumbles on an unburied coffin as he prepares to bed down for the night in a churchyard. [56] In the romance of *Sir Amadace*, in contrast, the knight traveling in a forest comes on a mysterious chapel lit by candles, and he must send first his servant, then his squire, and finally go himself before he can comprehend the inner scene: a lone, sorrowing mourner and a bier. [57] Again, when Eumenides and Jack arrive at the inn, instead of the helper's providing romance gifts—armor and a horse, as in *Sir Amadace* and *Olyver*—Jack offers the homely present of a purse filled with money for a meal at an inn, much as the red man provides the prince and himself with a simple breakfast, in "Beauty of the World." (The purse filled with money is itself a folktale motif.)[58]

One of Peele's most provocative manipulations of generic boundaries depends both on the thickness of romance and folktale's common boundary and the two genres' final distinction. As Gerould suggests, the hero of the Grateful Dead must often promise the magic helper to share any winnings, and at the penultimate moment, before the magic helper will reveal himself as the grateful spirit, he demands his half of the hero's gains. (Thus in *The Old Wives Tale,* after Eumenides has wakened Delia and been granted her hand, Jack reminds him, "You know you and I were partners, I to have halfe in all you got.") In the tale type, whether rendered in folktale or romance, the hero must respond by agreeing to "share" his wife (or child)—and thereby kill her—in order to fulfill his test and show his truth. However, because of their differing values, folktale and romance portray this action, the hero's response to the helper's demand, in contrasting ways. In *The Old Wives Tale*, the moment of Eumenides' response crystallizes, in an extraordinary suspension, both of these alternative portrayals.

56. "The King of Ireland's Son," in *Beside the Fire*, ed. Douglas Hyde (London, 1890), pp. 18–47; "Jack the Master and Jack the Servant," *Legendary Fictions of the Irish Celts,* ed. P. Kennedy (London, 1866), pp. 32–38.

57. *Sir Amadace and the Avowing of Arthur*, ed. Christopher Brookhouse, *Anglistica*, XV (Copenhagen, 1968), ll. 61–132.

58. This is the motif of the "magic purse," D1192.

In folktale, which focuses on the hero's achievement of his own potential, gaining possession of a woman with good qualities and status and making her a wife is part of the hero's self-realization; agreeing to "share" her at the helper's demand represents an ability to give up what he holds dear in order to further prove himself, his "truth." In romance the knight's truth is bound up with his vision of the woman; his quest for the ideal may be vested in a search for her, and she becomes—to use Eumenides' phrase—the "loadstar of his life." As a result, where folktale can stress the hero's ability to "come through," to make the choice at the helper's demand, for romance the moment is agonizing and almost irresolvable.

In "Beauty of the World," for example, the British folktale closest to Peele's promise, the hero responds with reluctance but with a clear sense of priorities. The red man, the magic helper, announces that his time for leaving has come:

> "I don't know what I'll do after you," said the king's son.
> "Oh, make no delay," said the red man; "the hire is just."
> "It is just," said the king's son.
> He made two halves of all he gained since he hired him. "I will give you my child all," said he; "I think it a pity to go to cut him in two."
> "I will not take him all," said the red man; "I will not take but my bargain."
> The king's son took a knife and was going to cut. "Stop your hand," said the red man.

In *Olyver of Castylle* when the hero falls on his knees before his wife, praying her to forgive him, she kisses him and begs God and the Virgin to forgive her husband if killing her should be a sin.[59] When he approaches her, he is like "a man halfe oute of his wytte." In Sir Amadace, the "dividing" of the woman is transmuted by constant references to the sacrifice of Christ, "þat me dere boȝte," on the part of the hero, his mistress, and even the magic helper, the White Knight.[60] In this romance the hero cannot resolve his dilemma, and it is his mistress "myld of mode" who precipitates the action by freely offering herself, in another loving sacrifice.

59. *The Hystorye of Olyver of Castylle*, pp. 329–334.
60. *Sir Amadace*, ll. 703 ff.

In *The Old Wives Tale* the moment before Jack's demand is sustained romance: Eumenides has wakened Delia and avowed his quest for the "fairest flower of these westerne parts." The princess has acknowledged him her knight and granted her love:

> Thou gentle knight, whose fortune is so good
> To finde me out, and set my brothers free,
> My faith, my heart, my hand, I give to thee.

(ll. 859–861)

With Jack's demand the play slips into folktale.

JACK

Why then maister draw your sworde, part your Lady, let mee have halfe of her presently.

EUMENIDES

Why I hope Jack thou doost but jest, I promist thee halfe I got, but not halfe my Lady.

JACK

But what else maister, have you not gotten her, therefore devide her straight, for I will have halfe, there is no remedie.

EUMENIDES

Well ere I will falsifie my word unto my friend, take her all, heere Jack ile give her thee.

JACK

Nay neither more nor lesse Maister, but even just halfe.

EUMENIDES

Before I will falsifie my faith unto my friend I will divide hir, Jacke thou shalt have halfe.

1 BRO.

Bee not so cruell unto our sister gentle Knight.

2 BRO.

O spare faire Delia, shee deserves no death.

EUMENIDES

Content your selves, my word is past to him, therefore prepare thy selfe Delya for thou must die.

DELIA

Then farewell worlde, adew Eumenides.

(ll. 886–903)

The exchanges have folktale's directness and lack of psychological rendering; the conflict for Eumenides, as for the prince of "Beauty," appears only in decisive, though changed, responses. But with the romance scene which precedes it, the folktale dialogue seems too quick, too casual, and too decisive. Eumenides' seems a shrug of resignation, Delia's a hasty adieu. The scene's possible romance version, with its idealization of the woman and the knight's elaborated, torturous difficulty, seems to accompany the dialogue as a faint reverberation, a missing possibility. Such an awareness of romance is reinforced by the Two Brothers, since they in fact express romance in the midst of folktale, as they plead for a vision of "faire Delia" and a "gentle Knight." It is no wonder that for Gwenan Jones the moment is perfect folktale and for Tucker Brooke it seems a parody of romance.[61] Eumenides' answer to Jack is both quite right and oddly, humorously, wrong; one genre is present, the other vibrates in the air. Unconventionally, this brief conventional scene reveals the incongruity in values of the two genres.

Such playful manipulations of genres may also suggest the rich variety with which fiction can seize human experience. The play is light and merry, and I am not proposing that it suggests the variety of human life of a Shakespeare play, with its intertwined human motives, the interaction of history and individual lives, or even the quick insights into character, Cleopatra's "I shall see / Some squeaking Cleopatra boy my greatness." Yet as *The Old Wives Tale* slips from one genre into another, crosses a generic boundary, it releases the audience from the confines of the first, its objects and tones, and suggests a new country with its new vision lying just beyond. The Harvesters' simple lyrics portray a male search for women in which human relationships are subsumed into nature's harmony and renewal: the men sow, the women bear "frute"; they claim a yearly cycle which leaps "mute" death to pass again into the quick and fertile. When their folk ritual shifts to romance, one man and one woman claim supreme earthly importance for each other, emotional desire mates with the physical, and nature dwindles to frozen obstacles and thorny beds. As folktale thrusts romance aside, it claims the need of men and women for gold and home, and offers a world of voices—for those who venture out—of animals and water, speaking and caressing, a nature animate with human emotion and sexuality re-embodied.

61. Gwenan Jones, p. 89; G. F. Tucker Brooke, p. 279.

From the beginning the play has been aware of fiction's power. Frolicke suggests its attraction in his eager hush, when the Characters appear: "Let them alone, let us heare what they will say," and the old storyteller awakens attention to fiction's rules by violating them with good-humored ease. Madge omits essential plot details ("O Lord I quite forgot, there was a Conjurer"), confuses her characters ("she [he I would say]") and refuses to choose their identities ("there was a King or a Lord, or a Duke"). The Characters appear onstage to tell their story better—in a manner like Pirandello's centuries later[62]—and their amiable storyteller is found asleep when they have finished. The tale seems to have a life, an autonomy, of its own, to go "rounde without a fiddling stick" as Frolicke says.

With the Harvesters, for their brief moments, an audience also seems to enter more deeply into a fictive life. There are no narrative threads to weave the figures into a familiar continuum of time and space; instead the audience is confronted and addressed directly. The Harvesters' metaphor of sowing and reaping is simple yet essential, the central point of their appearance, and it is directly presented. They are both closer to the audience than other characters and more fictive, and, momentarily, their pull into the circle transforms us into an audience resembling—not the confident group attending the *Knight of the Burning Pestle*—but rather the Grocer and his Wife, unsure of whether we are part of the stage's group or outside it.

It was once believed that such an artful structure, one of generic contrast created by a purposeful technique, would be beyond Peele's reach. In her study of "form in Elizabethan drama," for instance, Peele was one of Madeleine Doran's chief examples of an Elizabethan playwright seduced by a love of "abundant event" into creating plays of "shapeless unselectivity of incident."[63] There have been and still are great problems with Peele's texts, and even with their textual problems set aside, *Edward I* and *The Battle of Alcazar* remain episodic plays.[64] Nevertheless, the dramatic tech-

62. Allardyce Nicoll pointed out the resemblance to Pirandello (noted by Larsen, p. 165); Hook points out that Madge guesses wrong about the Harvesters' song, p. 427.

63. *Endeavors of Art* (Madison, Wis., 1954), p. 102.

64. See *Edward I*, ed. Frank S. Hook; *The Battle of Alcazar*, ed. John Yoklavich; *David and Bethsabe*, ed. Elmer M. Blistein, in *The Life and Works of George Peele*, ed. Prouty, II and III.

nique of *The Old Wives Tale* and the sensibility it requires accord with Peele's other works.

Recent studies by Inga-Stina Ewbank have persuasively argued for coherent structures in *David and Bethsabe* and *The Arraignment of Paris*.[65] In addition, she has suggested that to achieve these structures Peele deliberately employed techniques of abrupt reversal and contrast, techniques which resemble the shifts of *The Old Wives Tale*. For example, in order to portray "Paradise lost and regained" in *David and Bethsabe*, Peele created a structure with abrupt changes of mood for David, e.g., the King's brusque relinquishment of grief over his child's death, a sudden turn which can suggest David's change from helpless misery to a new conviction of grace.[66] For *The Arraignment*, Peele purposely contrasted the finale's joyful optimism with both the lament of Ate come from Hell, which opens the play, and the successive sorrows and forebodings of war which shadow the play throughout. As a result, the large and dramatic shift in mood celebrates the "mysterious power of royalty": "the wonder of the ending . . . is the defeat of a whole tragic and dynamic world order (its dynamism having provided the action of the play) by the simple, static presence of the queen."[67]

Complementary to these abrupt contrasts is Peele's fascination with replaying language and gesture with slight variations of form. A doubling of words (e.g., "all yee that lovely lovers be") is a hallmark of his phrases,[68] and a like repetition characterizes the pageant form in which he frequently wrote. Pageants more than plays or even masques are given to re-presenting an audience with images of itself, and such reflections may be double or even triple. Thus in Peele's *Descensus Astraeae*, a Lord Mayor's Show, one "web" is referred to in the Presenter's speech, another appears in a child's hands, and both are puns on the name of William Webbe, the

---

65. "The House of David in Renaissance Drama: A Comparative Study," *RenD*, VIII (1965), 3–40; and " 'What words, what looks, what wonders?' " in *The Elizabethan Theatre V*, ed. G. R. Hibbard (Hamden, Conn., 1975), pp. 124–154.

66. "The House of David," pp. 14–15, 21, 29, 38.

67. " 'What words, what looks,' " p. 138.

68. *Ibid.*, pp. 134–135. This repetition may ultimately derive, as Inga-Stina Ewbank suggests, from his attention to the match of word and spectacle, a sense that one doubles the other and need only point to it.

new mayor watching the pageant.[69] In the earlier *Pageant Borne before Wolstan Dixi*, a group of Londoners standing before Guildhall is faced first with "London" and then with a figure of London's "Loyaltie."[70] Such doubling becomes more dramatic in *The Arraignment*: the play centers first on the award of the apple and then replays that award, giving the prize to the queen of "a seconde Troie" (l. 1153).[71] This sense of reiteration is intensified by the play's attention to echo and refrain—the story of Echo is recited, lines of dialogue serve as lyrical refrains (e.g., ll. 382, 626 ff., 980), and the country gods "bestowe an Eccho" to a chorus until a choir echoes "within and without" (l. 166).

Yet more striking are Peele's playful repetitions in which the repeated form is slightly skewed or, the form unchanged, a new context creates an ironic difference. In *The Old Wives Tale*, for example, the repetition of the approach to the magic well is demanded by folktale, and conventionally the scene is unvaried until the moment when each sister shows her nature by responding differently to the Head. But instead of this strict repetition Peele changes both the song, by adding lines, and the physical appearance of the Head, e.g., by adding "eares of Corne." In a more general sense, the dramatic technique of the entire Tale consists, as we have seen, in repeating familiar conventions but changing them in odd ways, by a sudden suppression or a skewing of their form: the Golden Head chants and Zantippa responds with a blow, or Sacrapant is killed in not one but two different ways. Similarly, Peele emphasizes with a textual note a refrain in *The Arraignment* which is sung by a nymph and repeated by shepherds. In

---

69. *Descensus Astraeae*, ed. David H. Horne, in *The Life and Works of George Peele,* ed. Charles T. Prouty, vol. I. Bergeron notes the visual repetition in *English Civic Pageantry 1558–1642* (London, 1971), p. 136; Robert Withington notes the verbal in *English Pageantry* (Cambridge, Mass., 1920), II, 25. We have few details of the moment in which the shows were presented, but since speeches were directly addressed to the mayor (e.g., in Peele's Show of 1585), it seems safe to extend Withington's comment on the 1590 Show: "We may presume that the mayor stopped before the pageant to hear the speakers" (p. 25).

70. *Pageant Borne before Wolstan Dixi*, ed. David H. Horne, in *The Life and Works of George Peele*, ed. Prouty, vol. I. No setting for the spoken parts is named; the Guildhall as the place of arrival seems possible from von Wedel's description of the 1584 Lord Mayor's Show. See *Transactions of the Royal Historical Society*, N.S. IX (1895), 253–255.

71. *The Araygnement of Paris*, ed. R. Mark Benbow, in *The Life and Works of George Peele*, ed. Prouty, vol. III.

their mouths her words become a judgment on herself, an ironic "Ecco," caused by the changed context, which Peele points out as "the grace of this song."[72] In a like manner, near the end of *David and Bethsabe*, David addresses "faire Bersabe" (l. 1655), lauds her "sweet sight," and continues into a sustained praise of "beautie." His blazon is so like earlier reveries on Bethsabe that it comes as a shock when David explicitly names his subject as "faire peace" (l. 1668).[73] To underscore David's ability to look beyond earthly beauty, Peele has deliberately made the context ambiguous, played on the audience's sense of repetition, and then required a sudden re-framing and with it an awareness of the new and heavenly context.

The interest in fiction and its genres which is evident in *The Old Wives Tale* also characterizes both the ending of *The Arraignment*—with its deliberate move from fiction to reality, the Fates reaching forward to the Queen in the audience—and Peele's generic experimentation. *David and Bethsabe* is the only extant Elizabethan example of a "divine play"; it combines a religious theme with the techniques of a history play, taking the Bible as its chronicle source.[74] *The Arraignment* is known for synthesizing different styles and subject matters: R. Mark Benbow, the Yale editor, proposes pastoral, mythology, moralities, and masque among them.[75]

I would further suggest, without attempting to argue the point here, that the awareness of different genres which is required in order to combine them—as Peele does in *David and Bethsabe* and *The Arraignment*—demands a sensibility similar in kind and degree to that needed in order to contrast them—as he does in *The Old Wives Tale*. It would take another essay to propose that Elizabethan combinations of genre, as of comedy with tragedy, have been so visible and debated in literary history that these same combinations have silently—and mistakenly—been assumed to be

72. The Fates' reappearance and giving over of their instruments recalls the threat of Ate that Atropos is cutting the "threede of Troie."

73. The turn is indicated by "but" and a change of person, yet the intertwining of Bethsabe and "faire peace" is so skillful that for the moment of clarification Peele gives not only the name but an epithet, "goddesse of our graces here," to call attention to the change.

74. Lily B. Campbell, *Divine Poetry and Drama in Sixteenth Century England*, p. 260, referred to by Inga-Stina Ewbank, "The House of David," p. 5; and Elmer Blistein, Introduction, p. 175.

75. Benbow, Introduction, p. 26.

easier and more natural than the rarer contrast of genres. Here we may only note briefly the awareness of distinct tones and gestures suggested by the combination of *The Arraignment*. After Ate's appearance, for example, the gods who follow are disposed in a clear and careful progression: from country gods (as Pan), to earthly but more rarefied female divinities (as Flora), to the celestial goddesses (as Juno). The tone ranges from Rhanis's stately welcome of the goddesses to Juno's bickering with Venus; from the mourning over a shepherd dead for love to the bawdy of Vulcan and a nymph; from, finally, Ate's tragic lament to the rejoicing over Eliza. This variety, in its careful modulation, suggests a sensibility which—instead of gracefully blending the tones and gestures of pastoral, mythology, and "comedy of ideas"[76]—could equally well distill and sharpen generic moments, then gaily, abruptly, shift from one to another.

English dramatists of the 1580s and early 90s were faced with a wealth of plots, jokes, rhetorical styles, and genres; the comedies of George Peele and John Lyly suggest different approaches to this diversity. Each set a play in the English countryside, employed clever servants, an old woman, and magic. For *Mother Bombie* Lyly shaped, blended, and smoothed. He borrowed clever Roman plots, selected magic and riddling prophecy, then established them in Kent. The worldly sons of Terence and Plautus are softened to the adolescent heirs of wealthy farmers. Mother Bombie is an old woman who can see the future and interpret dreams, but her divination is lightened by common sense: asked to account for a fantastic dream, she suggests, "Belyke thou wentst supperlesse to bed."[77] Having molded a coherent bourgeois scene, Lyly then transmutes it to an impossibly articulate, rarefied world, peculiarly his own. The invention of wit springs forth at every sentence end; its phrasing, patterned and balanced, creates an extraordinary grace. Even the materialism of the fathers, for whom "marriage . . . is become a market," is distilled by a bargaining conducted in the elegant Lylian style.

76. "Comedy of ideas" is Benbow's term, p. 26.

77. *Mother Bombie*, ed. R. Warwick Bond, in *The Complete Works of John Lyly* (Oxford, 1902), vol. III. G. K. Hunter points out that both the specific portrayal of a bourgeois world and the lack of "shadow and the supernatural" are peculiar to *Mother Bombie* among Lyly's plays, in *John Lyly* (London, 1962), pp. 220–229. Yet the shadows, even when present, are of Lyly's own shaping; they are not direct imitations of folktale's Golden Heads. Lyly of course is writing for the boys and Peele for an adult company.

Peele in contrast selected and rendered in order to suggest both the variety of his sources and the intrinsic power of each. His old country-woman retorts in a hearty, vulgar style, "Heare my tale or kisse my taile"; divination is given to Erestus, an enchanted, riddling old man who becomes a bear at night. A ghost, a princess, and the magic Head appear, but lumbering into their midst come Wiggen and the good-natured Booby. The lyric Harvesters dance and sing of "reaping"; then Huanebango demands "ingresse and egresse . . . whosever saith no." A thunderous voice shouts "No," and the champion, in elegant slapstick, falls on his face.

As a result, *The Old Wives Tale* is pleasing partly for its simple "variety of spectacle" and its satisfaction of the old demands it embodies: a "Kinges Daughter" is rescued, generosity is rewarded, and lovers are reunited. [78] Yet in addition, unlike a Lyly comedy, a group of folktales, or even a self-conscious parody, Peele's play can awaken us to "the different levels of the imaginative life itself." [79] With its vivid incongruities, its vision of a Spanish braggart kneeling by the well of the water of life, *The Old Wives Tale* creates a passage through various fictions. As we change from folktale to romance to folk ritual, highly conventional forms removed from the everyday, tumble for an instant into the cynical or raucous and back, we seem to skate from one extraordinary possibility to another, to feel with delight the range of fiction.

78. Bradbrook, p. 325.

79. *Ibid.*, pp. 329–330. Goldstone proposes that the play is "dramatizing . . . the working of the imagination and showing how it enlarges, unifies, and yet refreshingly complicates human life," p. 213. I hope to have suggested the source of these perceptions. Earlier versions of this essay profited from the thoughtful criticisms of Phyllis Gorfain, Roberta Johnson, and the participants in David Bevington's NEH Seminar, 1978–79.

Role-Playing, Reflexivity, and Metadrama in Recent Shakespearean Criticism

MICHAEL SHAPIRO

WHEN NATASHA VISITS the opera in Tolstoy's *War and Peace* (VIII.ix), she responds to the literal, physical reality onstage rather than to the theatrical illusion: "She saw nothing but painted cardboard and strangely dressed-up men and women, talking, singing, and moving strangely about in the bright light. She knew what it all was meant to represent; but it was all so grotesquely false and unnatural that she felt alternately ashamed and amused at the actors."[1] By contrast, when Partridge attends a performance of Garrick's *Hamlet* in Fielding's *Tom Jones* (XVI.5), he responds to the events onstage as if they were happening in real life. At the closet scene, for example, he protests, "I know it is only a play," but nonetheless offers sympathy and encouragement to Hamlet and heaps his scorn upon Gertrude:

There, there—Ay, no wonder you are in such a passion; shake the vile wicked wretch to pieces. If she was my own mother, I would serve her so. To be sure, all duty to a mother is forfeited by such wicked doings. —Ay, go about your business, I hate the sight of you.[2]

Natasha and Partridge suggest conveniently opposed ways of looking at

1. Leo Tolstoy, *War and Peace*, trans. Constance Garnett (New York, 1931), p. 528.
2. Henry Fielding, *Tom Jones* (New York, 1950), p. 760.

drama. Preoccupied with her own problems, Tolstoy's heroine takes a position which had been more cogently developed by Dr. Johnson, while Fielding's bumbling ex-schoolmaster caricatures a point of view advanced by Coleridge. Johnson's conviction of spectators' constant awareness "that the stage is only a stage, and that the players are only players" implies considerable psychic distance from the dramatic illusion.[3] Although Coleridge's position—"We *choose* to be deceived"—assumes some awareness of the artifice involved in any dramatic illusion, an awareness which he even admits is essential for aesthetic pleasure, his ideal response is a state of rapt absorption in the work of art, as in a dream.[4] Whereas Johnson suggests a detached appreciation of the artistry exhibited in creating and sustaining the dramatic illusion, Coleridge implies that we engage ourselves emotionally with the illusion as if it were life: we feel the same feelings but do not act on those feelings. One might try to blur the differences between the two positions by characterizing the knowledge Johnson speaks of as "preconscious." We know it as we know our birthdays, telephone numbers, etc., but as we are conscious of possessing this knowledge only at such moments when it is brought to our attention, it usually does not interfere with our emotional acceptance of dramatic illusion. In the plays of Shakespeare and his contemporaries, however, the prevalence of self-reference brings this "preconscious" knowledge regularly to our awareness, and makes it harder to become absorbed solely in the representational or mimetic aspects of the play.

In our own century, scholars and critics have struggled to account for the ubiquity of illusion-shattering passages in Elizabethan drama. The work of three scholars provides a schematic outline of our progress. Over fifty years ago, Doris Fenton collected and categorized a large number of such passages in a study entitled *The Extra-Dramatic Moment in Elizabethan Plays Before 1616*, a useful catalog, hampered unfortunately by her own predisposition, betrayed in the title, to restrict drama to its mimetic

3. Samuel Johnson, "Preface to Shakespeare" (1765), in *Johnson on Shakespeare*, ed. A. Sherbo, in *Works* (New Haven, Conn., 1958——), VII, 77.

4. S. T. Coleridge, Lecture on *The Tempest* (1818–1819), in *Coleridge's Shakespearean Criticism*, ed. T. M. Raysor (Cambridge, Mass., 1930), I, 129. For a useful discussion of Coleridge's understanding of dramatic illusion, see R. H. Fogle, *The Idea of Coleridge's Criticism* (Berkeley, Calif., 1962), pp. 116–124.

dimension.[5] Toward the end of World War II, S. L. Bethell argued that Shakespeare's audiences inherited a habit of mind which enabled them to hold mimetic and presentational elements in suspension. "Dual consciousness," as he termed this quality, allowed them to see the actors both as actors and as characters simultaneously.[6] Within the last decade, Michael Goldman has asserted that our relationship with the actor is primary, a terrifying and thrilling encounter with "otherness," onto which is grafted character, plot, and all the other formal elements of drama.[7] Whereas Bethell gives equal weight to mimetic and presentational levels, Goldman considers dramatic texts primarily as vehicles for enriching and extending the ambivalences that result from confrontations with living actors.

In admitting this awareness of theatrical and dramatic artifice into critical discourse, both Bethell and Goldman typify a modern adaptation of the Johnsonian position, an adaptation surely influenced by current interest in reflexivity and self-consciousness in many forms of art. The Shakespearean criticism that is emerging from this set of concerns challenges both the Renaissance notion that art should conceal art and the naturalistic reduction of drama to mimesis. Earlier critics felt themselves somehow different from ordinary spectators in their curiosity about how various theatrical and dramatic effects were achieved. Probably underestimating audiences' delight in any display of technical virtuosity, they assumed that most spectators would suppress their awareness of the practical means which made the effect possible in order to preserve their emotional response to the dramatic illusion. With broader understanding of popular Renaissance theater and with naturalistic theory and practice in

5. Doris Fenton, *The Extra-Dramatic Moment in Elizabethan Plays Before 1616* (Philadelphia, 1930). For a sophisticated updating of this view, see Eugene Paul Nassar, "Shakespeare's Games with His Audience," in *The Rape of Cinderella* (Bloomington, Ind., 1970), pp. 100–119. Nassar divides Shakespeare's plays into a "core situation or action" (the dramatic illusion) and detached meditations given from a "choric posture" (p. 101).

6. S. L. Bethell, *Shakespeare and the Popular Dramatic Tradition* (Durham, N.C., 1944). In my book on the boy companies, *Children of the Revels* (New York, 1977), pp. 104 ff., it seemed obvious to me (and still does) that "dual consciousness" would be particularly strong when adult audiences were watching troupes of children performing in adult roles. Two reviewers have challenged this view: Kenneth Muir, "The boys on the boards," *TLS*, 3 February 1978, p. 111; and E. J. Jensen, *RenQ*, XXXI (1978), 247–249.

7. Michael Goldman, *The Actor's Freedom* (New York, 1975).

full flight, we find more and more critics like Bethell and Goldman
postulating spectators whose responses can encompass both dramatic illusion and theatrical reality.

From this perspective, most of Thomas F. Van Laan's *Role-playing in
Shakespeare* may seem something of a throwback to those modes of criticism which address themselves solely to the mimetic level of dramatic
literature. [8] Van Laan is cognizant, as we shall see, of reflexive tendencies
in Shakespeare and makes astute though sparing use of such passages, but
his main purpose is to describe the behavior of Shakespeare's characters in
histrionic terms: "Shakespearian man, whatever else he may be, is a role-
playing animal" (p. ix). For Van Laan, words like "act," "scene," "stage,"
"actor," "comedian," and their variants are usually not self-referential but
metaphoric. Rather than reminding us that we are watching or reading a
play, they nearly always establish role-playing as a central theme, alert us to
the characters' efforts at self-dramatization, or encourage us to note whether
the characters are violating or fulfilling their appropriate dramatic or social
roles.

The concept of role in Van Laan's hands is rich and subtle, ranging from
assigned parts in plays-within-plays, to "nonce" roles or temporary self-
projection, to dramatic roles assigned by the playwright, to social or
familial "office" (to use the Elizabethan term). While some characters
remain faithful to a single role, the more significant figures change roles or
turn out to be a "nexus" of discrete roles held simultaneously though not
necessarily equivalently. Despite Van Laan's careful definition of terms,
one fears that his approach will reduce the identity of dramatic characters
to their roles—whether single or aggregate—as social psychologists like
Erving Goffman have done for the human personality. While Van Laan sees
role as the essential determinant of identity (he is impatient with impres-
sionistic responses to the intangible "felt life" of characters), he is flexible
enough to consider "something that is independent of the character's roles
but nevertheless measured by them" (p. 40). Thus, the choice of roles, the
effects of change in role, the loss of role or threat of such loss, and the
manner of role-playing all point toward a dimension of identity that lies
beyond role, a dimension splendidly illuminated by Van Laan's discussions
of individual plays.

8. Thomas F. Van Laan, *Role-playing in Shakespeare* (Toronto, 1978).

One further aspect of identity arises, so Van Laan maintains, from "Shakespeare's tendency to fine excess in characterization" (p. 41), gratuitous utterances independent of role, such as Dogberry's speech beginning "Dost thou not suspect my place?" [9] An actor, to say nothing of spectators, readers, or critics, seeking the key to a character's identity might respond powerfully to just such details, especially if they are amplified linguistically or poetically. The key to Dogberry's identity, then, may not be his role as "bungling malapropian constable" (p. 41) but the fragile self-esteem of "a fellow that hath had lossess" (to quote from elsewehere in the same speech Van Laan cites). Shakespearean overabundance seems to me too facile an explanation for all details of character that elude Van Laan's notion of identity, a notion tied—however loosely—to role. Indeed, Van Laan elsewhere assumes a broader conception of identity, as when he explores the "discrepancies between characters and the parts they are called upon or choose to play" (p. 72) in plays like *Twelfth Night* and *Measure for Measure*.

In recent years it has become fashionable to describe characters as actors, stage managers, directors, playwrights, or even spectators. [10] For Van

9. *The Riverside Shakespeare*, ed. G. B. Evans (Boston, 1974), IV.ii.74 ff. Subsequent quotations from Shakespeare are from this edition.

10. For example, Lionel Abel, *Metatheatre* (New York, 1963), writes of characters like Hamlet and Falstaff as being aware of their own theatricality and hence of their superiority to their position in the play. In Prospero, Abel—like many others—sees such a character finally given the power his superior awareness implies—the power to dramatize others. As I understand him, Abel's theatrical metaphors are actually intended to describe a high degree of self-consciousness in a dramatic character. Marianne Novy, "Shakespeare's Female Characters as Actors and Audience," in *The Woman's Part: Feminist Criticism of Shakespeare*, ed. Carolyn Ruth Swift Lenz, Gayle Greene, and Carol Thomas Neely (Urbana, Ill., 1980), pp. 256–270, uses theatrical metaphors to contrast the heroines of the comedies with those of the tragedies. Whereas the former are forgiven for falsifying their identities in order to manipulate the men toward a happy resolution of the plot, the latter generally find themselves forced into the role of sympathetic audience to posturing, narcissistic heroes mistrustful of female pretense. In this position, heroines like Desdemona encourage the offstage audience to share their sympathy for the men they love, however misguided, resentful, or brutal those men become. Seeing characters as actors and spectators may have helped Novy to develop some illuminating contrasts between Shakespeare's comic and tragic heroines, but one wonders whether she might not have argued the differences more effectively without theatrical analogies, which also occur in the plays themselves, where they raise a host of issues unrelated to the feminist perspective.

Laan, however, acting or role-playing is not merely a convenient critical metaphor. Indeed, the strength of his book lies in his detailed support for the proposition that the concept of role-playing, "the essential theatrical quality of the real world" (p. 239), supplied Shakespeare with raw materials for the themes, structures, and plots of his plays over the course of his career. In the early comedies, Van Laan argues, Shakespeare developed a formal-thematic pattern in which nearly every character is brought to his ideal role through manipulative quasi-dramatic strategies, or "playlets," devised by himself or others. In some comedies, role-playing is explored thematically by the juxtaposition of several different types of role-players, as in *The Merchant of Venice*, where Antonio's reluctance to abandon his role of "the melancholic" is disconcertingly similar to Shylock's tenacious adherence to *his* role of "the Jew." In this play, as in *A Midsummer Night's Dream*, entire worlds can be characterized by their attitudes toward role-playing, as a fruitful tension develops between the rigidities of Venice or Theseus's court and the more fluid role-changes of Belmont and the Athenian Woods.

Similarly, the history plays through *Richard II* grow out of an opposition between unkingly kings, who may, like Richard II, know the language and gestures of true kingship without being able to fulfill the office, and would-be kings, the pretender-usurpers who can never get the role quite right, while the earlier tragedies, through *Hamlet*, focus on the failure of role-playing to control the complexities of experience, depicting the protagonists' futile efforts to project identities capable of defeating the hostile forces of chance, fate, history, or society. For artistic or personal reasons, the failure of role-playing began to impinge even on the middle comedies: *Twelfth Night* ends, so Van Laan argues, with Malvolio, Sir Andrew, and even Sir Toby (despite or because of his marriage to Maria) still fettered to the inappropriate selves they fashioned at the beginning of the play. In the problem plays, the bitter ironies surrounding the schemes of Vincentio in *Measure for Measure* and Helena in *All's Well* reflect and convey a lack of confidence in the possibility of human beings, unaided by higher powers, finding their own ideal roles or helping others to do so. Following a path first charted in the discussions of *The Comedy of Errors* and *Richard II*, Van Laan sees the major tragedies—*Othello, Macbeth,* and *Lear*—as a series of confrontations with the void that exists when all roles are lost—hero, lover, king, father, man. With literary tact and subtle compassion, Van Laan gauges the reactions of the tragic heroes to that emptiness—Othello's attempt to forge new roles, Macbeth's chilling description of spiritual desolation, and Lear's temporary recovery of his identity before its final obliteration. Van Laan finds *Coriolanus* and *Antony and Cleopatra*, concerned with the hero's failure to find an ideal setting for his role(s), less powerful as tragic statements, but sees anticipations of the late romances in the way Antony's failure to fuse his various roles is corrected in Cleopatra's vision of him, a vision created by her powerful imaginative projection of her own cluster of roles. Finally, Van Laan argues that the romances themselves stress the reacquisition of the same basic personal roles lost by the tragic heroes, through providential rather than human intervention.

These discussions, which have a grace and amplitude impossible to capture in my sketchy outlines, are firmly rooted in mimetic assumptions about drama: "the play constitutes at least in part a commentary on the real world by the dramatist" (p. 238). There are times, however, when Van Laan allows the self-referentiality of certain passages to lead him into the metadramatic speculation that the play is commenting on itself. In the discussion of *Julius Caesar*, for example, Van Laan stresses such passages as Cassius's and Brutus's meditation on future enactments of their "lofty scene," and concludes that Shakespeare "dramatizes not only the plight of his historical characters but also his own as a writer of historical drama" (p. 160). Similarly, when Troilus, Cressida, and Pandarus swear by their future reputations, which the audience knows to be worthless, Shakespeare defines them as actors playing parts written for them by history, parts which differ radically from their own conceptions of themselves, just as the Homeric figures we see squabbling, posturing, and intriguing have been ennobled by subsequent literary, historigraphical, and dramatic tradition.

In his closing pages, Van Laan's comments on *The Tempest* move from metadrama to metaphysics, as various elements of the play reveal themselves to be illusions contained within a higher reality. Thus, Prospero's masque is a contrivance in the play Prospero creates for the other characters, a play contained within Prospero's life, which his narrative reveals to have existed beyond the confines of the play we are watching. However, as the epilogue indicates, Prospero is merely a character at the audience's and Shakespeare's level of reality, though even that reality may from a higher point of view be merely an "insubstantial pageant," a thought which may underlie the epilogue's sudden turn from plaudite to prayer. Like the comments on *Julius Caesar* and *Troilus and Cressida*, the section on *The Tempest* assumes that references to theatrical reality are less concerned to evoke the histrionic behavior of human beings in everyday life than to make us consciously aware of broader resemblances between life and theater. If Van Laan is right about the importance of self-referentiality in these plays, as I think he is, one would expect other critics less committed to mimetic presuppositions than he to find it in other plays, where he assures us it does not exist.

Such indeed is the case, as a good deal of Shakespearean criticism of the past twenty years can attest. In fact, the issue is no longer the presence or even the amount of reflexivity in the works of Shakespeare and other Elizabethan dramatists, but rather its significance. Here one has a number of competing or complementary theories to consider, most of them developed out of readings of Shakespeare but surely applicable in various ways to his contemporaries.

One function of reflexivity is to control the audience's degree of involvement in the stage illusion. About twenty years ago, Maynard Mack contended that through verbal and spatial reminders of theatrical reality Shakespeare brought the world of the actors or the audience into his plays at moments when he wished to increase spectators' psychic distance from the action—to forestall an emotional or critical response or to encourage analysis or reflection. [11] In other places, explicit allusion to theatrical reality, especially plays-within-plays, has the opposite effect of lending depth and substantiality to the stage illusion, as *The Murder of Gonzago* does to Claudius's court in *Hamlet*.

A related use of reflexivity involves a more active interplay between different planes of illusion than in the example from *Hamlet*. As Robert Weimann has argued, the popular clowning tradition bequeathed to the Elizabethan theater a style of performing designed to achieve extremely close rapport with audiences. Actor-characters using such techniques as

11. Maynard Mack, "Engagement and Detachment in Shakespeare's Plays," in *Essays on Shakespeare and the Elizabethan Drama in Honour of Hardin Craig,* ed. R. Hosley (London, 1963), pp. 280–285.

direct address, real or feigned improvisation, downstage playing, linguistic inversion, topical allusion, and parodic imitation could set off their own heightened theatrical reality against other, more mimetic or illusionary aspects of a play, as Will Summers does in *Summer's Last Will and Testament*. [12]

A third function of reflexivity is to add various kinds of resonances to spectators' responses to any given dramatic illusions. Two essays in *Shakespeare: The Theatrical Dimension*, for example, assuming a measure of implicit self-referentiality in Elizabethan stage production, argue that Shakespeare's audience could not have failed to register certain theatrical realities and that Shakespeare made artistic use of this awareness.

In "Some Dramatic Techniques in *King Lear*," William H. Matchett writes as if he were an Elizabethan Natasha seeing the play for the first time and consistently being misled to expect a happy ending, as in the earlier non-Shakespearean version of the story. [13] Elaborating an insight first made by Harry Levin over twenty years ago, Matchett argues that Shakespeare's bare stage would not have permitted such a naïve spectator to know whether or not Gloucester was supposed to be standing on the cliffs of Dover. Edgar describes the heights in the same fashion as real place settings are described in Shakespeare, and while one trusts that Edgar intends his father no harm, the outcome of the suicide attempt remains as much in doubt as the precise locale. This doubt, made possible only by a conscious awareness of the theatrical reality, is dispelled only with Edgar's lines,

> Had he been where he thought,
> By this had thought been past,
>
> (IV.vi.44–45)

12. Robert Weimann, *Shakespeare and the Popular Tradition in the Theater*, trans. R. Schwartz (Baltimore, 1978).

13. William H. Matchett, "Some Dramatic Techniques in *King Lear*," in *Shakespeare: The Theatrical Dimension*, ed. Philip C. McGuire and David A. Samuelson (New York, 1979), pp. 185–208. Matchett also employs the perspective of "the naïve spectator" in "Some Dramatic Techniques in 'The Winter's Tale,'" *ShS*, XXII (1969), 93–107, where he points out the usefulness of the ambiguities created by the audience's initial realization that Hermione's statue was being represented by the same actress who played the living Hermione.

and Matchett goes on to argue that the relief one feels here is yet another of the play's deceptive moves toward "comfort, revelation and reconciliation" (p. 189).

In similar fashion, Steven Booth's essay, "Speculations on Doubling in Shakespeare's Plays," hypothesizes the kinds of effects Shakespeare might have achieved *if* certain roles, such as Cordelia and the Fool, were doubled, and *if* such doubling was apparent to the audience. [14] The second condition seems less controversial than the first for the leading repertory company of a small city performing by daylight. As to the likelihood of such doubling, Booth cites known evidence of the practice assembled by Bevington and others, but admits he can prove nothing about specific instances in Shakespeare. Yet in examining the arguments against the use of doubling by Shakespeare's troupe advanced by Lawrence, Ringler, Thaler, and others, Booth demonstrates those arguments to be just as speculative as his own, based as they are on dubious suppositions about Elizabethan actors (i.e., that they generally disliked doubling roles and preferred to stick to their "lines" unless forced by necessity to add one or more roles) and audiences (i.e., that they preferred not to notice an actor displaying his virtuosity in two or more roles). It remains to be seen whether such a fresh view of the theatrical viability of doubling will stimulate scholars to find evidence for specific instances in Shakespeare. More generally, Booth's essay is an invitation to scholars to explore other manifestations of Shakespeare's ingenious interplay "between our consciousness of the events portrayed and our consciousness of the actual theatrical events that convey the story" (p. 103).

Reflexivity can also add resonance to a play by reminding the audience that life too is a play, not simply with respect to the role-playing Van Laan describes, but in the sense that human beings participate in a transitory illusion witnessed, if not created, by God. Scholars such as Thomas Stroup have studied various interpretations of the *Theatrum mundi* topos and its influence on dramatic form. [15] In *The Theater and the Dream*, Jackson Cope has explored the philosophical and religious implications of reflexivity by

14. Stephen Booth, "Speculations on Doubling in Shakespeare's Plays," in *Shakespeare: The Theatrical Dimension*, pp. 103–131.

15. Thomas B. Stroup, *Microcosmos: The Shape of the Elizabethan Play* (Lexington, Ky., 1965).

examining the influence of Florentine Platonism on Renaissance drama. [16]
Like dreams, he argues, plays are evanescent and trivial as well as profound
and prophetic. Through visual and verbal reflexivity, plays proclaim their
theatricality, yet they transcend their own artificiality by showing us
truths deeper than anything mimesis can reflect back at us, deeper than
anything our social order can contain. By enlisting our imaginative participation in its "visible metaphors" (a term Cope borrows from Ortega y
Gasset) of the realm beyond reality, the theater grants us too a moment of
self-transcendence. However involved these epistemological puzzles become, as in plays containing plays or dreams, Cope believes that they are
inseparably linked to the tradition of self-referentiality we find all through
Renaissance drama.

Another function of reflexivity is to underscore what has been called the
metadramatic or metatheatrical aspect of plays, the proposition that plays
are in part at least about themselves, some aspect of dramatic or theatrical
art, or the responses of spectators. In some cases, these concerns blend, as
in recent attempts to describe how Shakespeare's plays convey to their
audiences the playwright's belief in the social value of dramatic illusions.
In *Shakespeare and the Idea of the Play*, Anne Righter [Barton] tried to
determine Shakespeare's attitude toward playing from his use of theatrical
metaphors, which he occasionally expanded into internal plays. Moreover,
she also defined, but left for others to elucidate, "the undeclared play
within the play, dramatic illusions created within the structure of life itself
which lead the unsuspecting to confuse artifice with reality." [17] In *Drama
Within Drama*, a study of *King Lear*, *The Winter's Tale*, and *The Tempest*,
Robert Egan argues that the imaginative participation of internal audiences to such undeclared playlets is a model for the offstage audience: e.g.,
Leontes' surrender to Camillo's and then Paulina's quasi-dramatic artifices
suggests that receptive spectators absorbing the artist's vision can transform human reality into the image of their desires. [18]

Anthony B. Dawson maintains roughly the same position in *Indirections:
Shakespeare and the Art of Illusion*, but lays far greater stress than Egan does

---

16. Jackson I. Cope, *The Theater and the Dream* (Baltimore, 1973).

17. Anne Righter [Barton], *Shakespeare and the Idea of the Play* (London, 1962), p. 144.

18. Robert Egan, *Drama Within Drama* (New York, 1975).

on reflexivity. [19] Dawson believes that Shakespeare underscores the patent theatricality of the undeclared internal plays created through such devices as "deceit, disguise, and manipulation" by characters who function as directors, playwrights, or stage managers. No one will be surprised to find Dawson concluding that such devices lead to self-knowledge in the early and middle comedies, that Shakespeare dramatized their inadequacy to bring enlightenment to worlds beset with pressing moral or political dilemmas in the problem plays and in some tragedies, and that in further emphasizing their artificiality when he returned to them in the late romances, he implied that life itself was no less illusory. Neither do Dawson's discussions of individual plays contain many surprises, although he has some cogent remarks on *All's Well* and *Measure for Measure*, where Shakespeare seems to have extended his usual comic structures beyond their range. Dawson might have included a chapter on *Much Ado*, with its plethora of internal playlets developed by characters wishing to deceive or manipulate others, or some commentary on the histories, which also involve deceit and manipulation. Unfortunately, Dawson's restricted selection of plays prevents us from learning whether the success or failure of internal, quasi-dramatic illusions to provide moral illumination is a function of genre or of Shakespeare's psychological and artistic development, or some combination of these and other factors. Comic conventions, one must concur, do usually lead to happiness in comedy and to grief in tragedy. Moreover, Dawson blurs important differences when he stretches terms like "deceit" and "manipulation" to cover the varieties of illusion created by such diverse characters as Portia, Rosalind, Helena, Vincentio, Hamlet, Edgar, Cleopatra, and Prospero, and in some instances tacitly abandons his assertion that such illusions are presented reflexively. Nor can his approach accommodate the explicit self-referentiality that comes through Shakespeare's plays even when there are no internal illusions. In short, the linkage of undeclared playlets with reflexivity will not support the weight of the metadramatic meditations on the moral value of theater which Dawson finds in the plays.

Alvin B. Kernan discovers similar meditations in *The Playwright as Magician*, but sets them on a broader foundation than Dawson does by

19. Anthony B. Dawson, *Indirections: Shakespeare and the Art of Illusion* (Toronto, 1978).

seeing them as outgrowths of Shakespeare's justification of his craft, a justification in part evoked by his own grave doubts about the value of playing. The book's subtitle, *Shakespeare's Image of the Poet in the English Public Theater*, indicates the nature of the doubts. [20] Anxious about his own social and moral position, Shakespeare on the one hand could see himself as a poet—a calling whose status was certified by Petrarch, Castiglione, and Sidney—on the other hand as a purveyor of ephemeral public entertainment for inept actors and rowdy audiences. On the one hand, he could be dazzled by the potential power of drama to reveal or transform reality; on the other, he could wince at the actual conditions under which his work was performed. Kernan discerns both tendencies in the internal playlets he discusses, as well as in some of the "undeclared" plays-within-plays, and so modifies the self-disparaging Shakespeare that emerges from Anne Righter [Barton]'s study of his explicit theatrical imagery.

Kernan further argues that Shakespeare made artistic capital out of this tension between his skepticism of his craft and his commitment to it. In *Hamlet*, for example, this tension surfaces in the difference between the mimetic-didactic theories of drama Hamlet articulates in the "mirror-up-to-nature" passage, and the passages, such as the Player King's speech in *The Murder of Gonzago*, which remind us that life—onstage as well as off—is as theatrical as a play—"ambiguous, changing, transient" (p. 106). In *King Lear*, Kernan emphasizes the playlets devised by Edgar and Cordelia; however nobly intended to heal their fathers' wounded spirits, these "morality plays" cannot prevent, contain, or even explain the agonized suffering of the play's final act. In *The Tempest*, as in *A Midsummer Night's Dream*, Kernan finds Shakespeare using metadramatic means to make what has become a familiar metaphysical point: "If *all* the world is a play, then one play may be as true as another" (p. 78). Kernan first sees self-referentiality in Shakespeare as self-mockery, one half of a deep ambivalence about the value of theater, but ends up considering it as the vehicle for a religious interpretation of *Theatrum mundi* which he puts succinctly: "Plays are not real, but then neither is the world itself" (p. 145). Perhaps a fuller treatment of the problem might plot the curve of this change over Shakespeare's career and seek explanations for it.

Although James L. Calderwood's *Metadrama in Shakespeare's Henriad*,

20. Alvin B. Kernan, *The Playwright as Magician* (New Haven, Conn., 1979).

like Kernan's book, investigates Shakespeare's skepticism of his medium, it focuses primarily on language and only secondarily on theater. [21] Calderwood reads the second tetralogy, in part, as a meditation on the political and artistic consequences of "the fall of speech," the change from a language thought to be based on God-given bonds between words and things to one in which words acquire arbitrary meanings. Readers of Calderwood's earlier book, *Shakespearean Metadrama* (1971), will recognize this change as the central issue of its final chapter on *Richard II*, and will find the same material serving as the starting point of the present volume. But whereas the earlier book surveyed a different metadramatic issue in each of a handful of plays, the present volume offers a tightly cohesive argument about the kinds of truth kings and playwrights can achieve when they use, as they must, a corrupt and lie-ridden language.

Historical discussion of language is reserved for an appendix entitled "Elizabethan Naming," where Calderwood outlines a shift in attitudes toward language that occurred during the sixteenth and seventeenth centuries. He characterizes this shift as a movement from verbal realism to verbal skepticism, from a belief in the congruity between language and reality to a despair in the power of language accurately to reflect the world, and cites the pressures of both empiricists and Puritans for stylistic simplicity as indexes and partial causes of this loss of faith. Recognizing that Shakespeare's plays precede the texts that most clearly articulate this shift, Calderwood argues that the playwright somehow discerned and reflected the trend in the second tetralogy as it was happening:

From his own deep engagement with language Shakespeare evidently *sensed a subliminal drift* of culture that was not to become publicly manifest until the science and philosophy of the seventeenth century. . . .

(p. 193)

The words I have italicized suggest a perspicacity one would hesitate to deny to Shakespeare, but which could also cover a multitude of anachronisms. Whereas most readers will accept Calderwood's general account of changes in attitudes toward language, and of the corresponding collision of verbal styles in *Richard II*, both of which have been frequently observed by

---

21. James L. Calderwood, *Metadrama in Shakespeare's Henriad* (Berkeley, Calif., 1979).

others, some may object that Calderwood imposes this pattern too neatly on the entire *Henriad*, while others may question his extension of it to the dramatist's skepticism of theatrical form.

If the conceptual underpinnings of the book are not as strongly cross-braced as one might wish, its critical thrust is nevertheless genuinely exciting. Calderwood's argument may for convenience' sake be divided into two parallel streams. On the political level, *The Henriad* traces the corruption of public discourse to the collapse of a sacramental, ontological language in *Richard II*, where Richard at least regards "the king" and his own identity as one indissoluble entity, despite his own unkingly conduct. His discovery of their separability reduces him to nothing. Richard's view is not, of course, Shakespeare's and the play advances a diametrically opposing view through Bolingbroke, whose sense of language is pragmatic and fluid and for whom the title of king follows the shiftings of political power. But Bolingbroke is in constant danger of being hoist with his own linguistic petard. Indeed, his debasement of language legitimizes the politic lie (e.g., John's "promise" of amnesty to the rebels in the Gaultree Forest) and the possibility of other kings—no less counterfeit than he (e.g., Mortimer, Hotspur)—and makes him vulnerable to parody by the most flagrant and shameless liar of them all—Falstaff, "the corporealized lie" (p. 68). For Hal, the problem is to become a genuine king in this world of lies. Even before his father's death, which allows him to inherit the crown legitimately despite his father's usurpation of it, he has begun to acquire the qualities which will enable him to wear it with some justification. Upon his accession, he skillfully assumes the regal role, and possesses it with even greater theatrical vitality than the diminished Falstaff does by the end of Part II. In *Henry V* Hal struggles to master the many facets of that role and must even pass an ordeal by combat uncertain of God's help, yet he can stand aside from the ceremonial trappings of sovereignty when need be. He substitutes "for inherent validity an achieved validity" (p. 179), and so partially redeems language from its fallen state.

As a commentator on Shakespeare's understanding of history and politics, Calderwood's observations are shrewd but not strikingly novel. More impressive is his contention that Shakespeare uses the historical and political surface of the plays as a metaphor for his own artistic struggles. Only through metaphor, Calderwood argues, can an artist use a lie-ridden language to approach truth. Just as Hal must enact the false role of wastrel prince in order to buttress his true role of Henry V, so must Shakespeare use the falsehoods of theatricality to dramatize the truth of history. Falstaff, the lie made flesh which Shakespeare added to history, is also the incarnation of theatricality—the embodiment of a view which reduces both history and the mimetic mode used to dramatize it to mere artifice. As a threat to political and artistic unity, Falstaff must be bought off, and so Hal gilds the lie Falstaff tells about Hotspur's death. Indeed, he is indispensable, for "if theatrical illusion is a lie, it is a lie that must be countenanced, for there can be no theater without it" (p. 80). Falstaff's part of the bargain is to relinquish the more overt forms of his theatricality, to live in the world of history, and so in Part II he withers and pales noticeably.

In a particularly fine chapter, Calderwood reads Part II as a withered and pale repetition of Part I, politically and dramatically vitiated by the high cost of maintaining Lancastrian order. Hal, on the other hand, retains sufficient theatricality to control the kingdom and the play *Henry V* by self-dramatization, to weld the diverse ingredients of both into a unified epic whole, while Shakespeare, through the Chorus, repeatedly reminds us of the theatrical lies used to convey this illusion of historical reality and hence of the collaborative nature of both his and Henry's audiences in the theatrical and political enterprises that constitute the play.

Calderwood's handling of Shakespeare's political and artistic concerns is less compartmentalized and far more subtle in detail than my summary suggests. The writing is deft and lively, and one admires his boldness in approaching something other than comedy with an awareness of theatrical artifice. But his restricting his argument to *The Henriad* raises questions about its validity. If Shakespeare was as preoccupied with the fall of speech and the theatrical uses of lying as Calderwood believes, surely there must be traces of these preoccupations in other plays written in or near the years (1595–1599) during which he composed the second tetralogy. (In fact, the very cohesiveness of Calderwood's argument implies a similarly cohesive design for this set of four plays, a cohesiveness that might have been difficult for Shakespeare to maintain during a period when he was also writing other plays.) Had Shakespeare been obsessed with the problems Calderwood investigates in *The Henriad*, one would expect to encounter

similar meditations on language and theater, at least in the middle comedies and early tragedies, although wherever they are found a skeptic might
attribute them to the critic rather than the dramatist. I suspect we need
much more metadramatic analysis of the entire Shakespearean canon before
anything like a rough consensus emerges as to which concerns were para-
mount in which plays, and how central they are to our critical responses,
just as we need more metadramatic readings of other Elizabethan plays in
order to set Shakespearean metadrama in its historical context.

Whereas Egan, Dawson, and Kernan agree that metadramatic readings
of Shakespeare will reveal his attitudes toward the value of theater,
Calderwood's metadramatic readings of *The Henriad* point to concerns
about quite different aspects of dramatic art. Dismissing these readings as
projections of the critic's own preoccupations is no more or less valid than
it is with any other critical readings. Nor is diversity of results from a
common approach any more of a problem for metadramatic critics than for
critics of other persuasions, who also bring to each text their own unique
sensibilities and personal histories along with whatever ideological equip-
ment they share. Metadramatic criticism too will stand or fall in each case
depending on whether the particular artistic concerns discovered accord
with the facts of the work of art and how much light they shed on those
facts. It has a major advantage over other critical modes, however: it
addresses those facts of dramatic art which have too often been excluded
from critical discourse, those facts arising from our awareness of the
physical conditions of playing. In accepting this awareness of theatrical
reality as a legitimate part of the critical response, metadramatic criticism
promises a way of responding to both artifice and illusion at once. It may
never marry Natasha to Partridge, or Johnson to Coleridge, but it can
bring them into effective alignment.

Notes on Contributors

ANNETTE DREW-BEAR teaches English at the University of California, Santa Barbara, and has written *Rhetoric in Ben Jonson's Middle Plays* and an essay on Jonson's face-painting scenes for *Studies in Philology*.

MARJORIE GARBER, Professor of English at Harvard University, is the author of *Dream in Shakespeare*, articles on Shakespeare, Marlowe, and Milton, and, most recently, *Coming of Age in Shakespeare*.

R. B. GRAVES is an Assistant Professor of Theater at the University of Illinois and has published essays on the staging and lighting of Elizabethan plays in *Renaissance Drama*, *Theatre Notebook*, and *Shakespeare Studies*.

ROBERT HELLENGA is an Associate Professor of English at Knox College. He has published two short stories and a number of articles in academic journals, and is currently working on an article on reader-response criticism. The original version of "Elizabethan Dramatic Conventions and Elizabethan Reality" was written for an NEH Seminar at the University of Chicago.

JOAN C. MARX is a Lecturer at Stanford University. She has published an essay on *Cymbeline*'s contrast of genres and is presently at work on a study of the Player's Speech in *Hamlet*.

MICHAEL SHAPIRO is an Associate Professor of English at the University of Illinois and the author of *Children of the Revels: The Boy Companies of*

163

Shakespeare's Time and Their Plays. He is currently working on self-conscious theatricality in Shakespeare's histories and tragedies.

MARION TROUSDALE, Associate Professor of English at the University of Maryland, has written articles on Renaissance and modern drama, including an essay on Harley Granville-Barker which appeared in Volume IV of *Renaissance Drama*. She is the author of *Shakespeare and the Rhetoricians*.